汉英对照
CHINESE-ENGLISH

MEDITATIVE NOTES IN SOLITUDE

小窗幽记

［明］陈继儒　　　/　著
周文标　　　　　/　英译
周文标　应佳鑫　/　译注

百花洲文艺出版社
BAIHUAZHOU LITERATURE AND ART PRESS

图书在版编目（CIP）数据

小窗幽记：汉英对照 /（明）陈继儒著；周文标英译；周文标，应佳鑫译注.
-- 南昌：百花洲文艺出版社，2020.9
ISBN 978-7-5500-3782-3

Ⅰ.①小… Ⅱ.①陈…②周…③应… Ⅲ.①人生哲学 – 中国 – 明代②《小窗
幽记》– 译文 – 汉、英③《小窗幽记》– 注释 – 汉、英 Ⅳ.①B825

中国版本图书馆CIP数据核字（2020）第131985号

小窗幽记：汉英对照

XIAO CHUANG YOU JI: HAN-YING DUIZHAO

[明] 陈继儒 著　周文标 英译　周文标　应佳鑫 译注

出 版 人	章华荣
责任编辑	郝玮刚　蔡央扬　程慧敏
书籍设计	方　方
制　　作	周璐敏
出版发行	百花洲文艺出版社
社　　址	南昌市红谷滩新区世贸路898号博能中心A座20楼
邮　　编	330038
经　　销	全国新华书店
印　　刷	江西华奥印务有限责任公司
开　　本	787mm × 1092mm 1/16　印张 14.25
版　　次	2020年9月第1版第1次印刷
字　　数	219千字
书　　号	ISBN 978-7-5500-3782-3
定　　价	56.00元

赣版权登字 05-2020-110

邮购联系 0791-86895109
网　址 http://www.bhzwy.com
图书若有印装错误，影响阅读，可向承印厂联系调换。

走向世界的明清小品
——汉英对照本"处世三奇书"序

The Sketches of the Ming and Qing Dynasties Going Abroad
— Preface to the "Three Canons of Personal Cultivation"

赵丽宏
Zhao Lihong

"处世三奇书"是中国古典文学的汉英对照本。在中国传统文化的出版物中，这是一套体例新颖的双语读本。这个读本，不仅向读者展现了中国古典文学一方迷人的天地，也为对中国文化有兴趣的英语读者提供了一个学习的园圃。读者可以由中文而英文，也可以由英文而中文。研习英文的中国读者，学习中文的外国读者，都可以在其中获得阅读的乐趣。

"Three Canons of Personal Cultivation" is a Chinese-English version of Chinese classical literature. In the publications of Chinese traditional culture, this is a set of bilingual readings with new style. It not only shows the charming world of Chinese classics, but also provides a learning garden for English readers who are interested in Chinese culture. Readers can read the canons in two ways, either from Chinese to English or from English to Chinese. Both Chinese readers who are learning English and foreign readers who are learning Chinese are enabled to get the pleasure of reading them.

《菜根谭》《小窗幽记》和《围炉夜话》是明清时期流传下来的三本以修身养性、劝善励志为中心话题的清言体小品集，作者分别是洪应明、陈继儒和王永彬。因其在同类书中出众的地位和影响力，被世人誉为"处世三奇书"，颇受文人墨客和普通百姓的喜爱。

The Roots of Wisdom, Meditative Notes in Solitude and *Fireside Talk at Night* are the three famous books successively appearing in the Ming Dynasty (1368-1644) and the Qing Dynasty (1644-1911), with subjects mainly on moral cultivation and inspirational exhortations on doing good and working hard, and therefore known as the "Three Canons of Personal Cultivation" out of their unparalleled status in books of the same kind and influence among the intellectuals and ordinary people.

华夏文化的发展，每个历史时期都有创造性的文学形态，并在各自领域中登峰造极，成为一个时代的文化标记。明清两朝也不例外，在前后五个多世纪里，小说显然是明清时期的一个主要文化特色，其次就是那些饱蕴着智慧才情、展示着世态风情的辑录和承载着先人学说和思想的格言体小品集了。通过这些作品，我们可以清楚地了解到：优秀的文学家，是中国传统文化的脊梁，他们那些形诸文字的精神与情感结晶是中华文明最有生命力的一部分。世风日下依然能倡导并坚持孝悌，物欲横流依然能淡泊名利，仕途得意依然能心存忧患意识，遭遇不测依然能泰然处之，国家危亡依然能竭尽忠诚，温饱之余依然能不忘劳作之苦，生活清贫依然能寄情山水，凡此种种，都是这些优秀文人留给后世的宝贵精神财富。

In the long history of China, cultural development of each era has its own creative literary form and insurmountable height, thus becoming a cultural mark of the time, the same those of the dynasties of Ming and Qing. During more than five centuries, the novels and fictions are of course the primary literary identity of the dynasties, and the collections brimming with human wits and revealing the ways of the world and the compilations of previous classical works, ancestors' quotes and their developed writings must be the next. Through these works and writings, we see clearly that the excellent literati are really the backbone of Chinese classical culture, and that the crystallization of spirit and emotion they created in words is one of the most vivid parts of Chinese civilization. As the breeders of the civilization of that times, even when the general moves were getting worse and worse they would remain faithful to filial piety and fraternal duty;

even when in an acquisitive time they would remain indifferent to fame and wealth; even when content with their official careers they would remain preoccupied with the misery consciousness; even when coming across unexpected occurrences they would remain unruffled and take them calmly; even when the state was in peril they would remain loyal; even when having enough food and clothing they would remain concerned about the pain of labor; even when living a poor life they would remain disposed to bask in the poetic mood between mountains and rivers. — All these refined qualities are the precious spiritual wealth the excellent literati handed down to us later generations.

"处世三奇书"所收纳的短句小品均为清言体，风格相似，读起来朗朗上口，既有诗歌的韵律又有散文的流畅。这些编辑成集、主题鲜明的短句小品，是被柔美化了的格言，似诗非诗，似文非文，是小品文的一种，形式上是介于箴言警句和散文之间的文体，通常由前后对仗或排比的两句或两段组成，以达到均衡与和谐之美。由清言汇集而成的书籍叫清言集或清言体小品集，有分编和不分编两种，题材自由，体例松散，所收清言小品数量少则近百则、多则数百则不等，每则小品的篇幅少则七八个字，多则逾百。内容涵盖古贤经典和民俗文化，其中尤以演绎儒道释三家之言为多，形式短小精致，文风飘逸清雅，具有"小品中的小品（林语堂语）"的美称。

The short sketches contained in the "Three Canons of Personal Cultivation" are all with distinctive themes, clear-spoken, similar in style, easy to read, and full of the rhythm of poetry and fluency of prose. So far as the form is concerned, these sketches belong to a kind of maxims literarily beautified with a manner of seemingly like but actually not a poem or seemingly like but actually not a prose, normally composed of two sentences or two paragraphs adorned with antitheses, couplets and other rhetoric devices to achieve the beauty of balance and harmony, and with its writing style lying between maxim and prose. The collections with such writings are called clear-and-upright sketches, usually there being two ways of compilation, classified or non-classified, either freely with subject matter or loose in layout, in which the pieces collected vary from nearly one hundred to several hundreds, and Chinese characters used in different pieces vary from seven or eight to more than a hundred, and the contents arranged cover Chinese classics and folk culture, mostly related to the sayings derived from the theories of Confucianism, Taoism and Buddhism. They are short in length, vivid in format and elegant in expression, and therefore praised by Mr. Lin Yutang (a famous modern Chinese scholar) as "a mini-sketch of sketches".

"处世三奇书"的可贵之处在于：三位作者皆以其丰富的学养、渊博的知识、明敏的思辨、冷隽的文字、促人深省的儆诚、益人心智的启迪，以及豁达如禅的觉醒，从古贤经典和民俗文化中撷取菁华但又不简单地复述这些原文，而是在赋予它们一定的情景衬托后将其锻造成一个个既养眼又养心的段子，于寥寥隽语中将经典所含的意旨优雅地展现在读者面前，充分诠释了中国传统文人的文化底蕴和人文情怀，为世人展现了一幅古人修身养性的清晰图景，让读者在诵读这些金科玉律时多了一份愉悦感和亲近感。

The praiseworthiness of the "Three Canons of Personal Cultivation" is as obvious as this: instead of simply quoting the original sayings, the three authors, by applying their rich learning and cultivation, profound knowledge, dialectical thinking, grave and stern expressions, thought-provoking warning, meditative enlightenment and self-awareness, turned out their sketches in the least paradoxes to exemplify the extracts from the classical works and folk culture, and gave prominence to the pieces well matched with relevant scene, sight, circumstances, background or landscape, thus achieving the effect of being pleasant to readers' eyes and minds. Their endeavors fully annotate the cultural deposits and humanistic sensibilities of the traditional literati, and thus enable us to have the opportunity to see a clear picture of the personal cultivation of the ancients, and make us feel more pleasure and intimacy than ever in reading the famous aphorisms of ancient classics.

　　十年前，周文标先生在上海人民出版社出版发行《菜根谭》汉英对照本时，我曾为他写过一篇序。据我所知，十余年来，他一直不懈地致力于用英文翻译和编撰中国传统典籍，并在呈现方式上做了积极的探索。这次他与百花洲文艺出版社共同成套推出"处世三奇书"汉英对照本，足见他这些年在这方面所倾注的时间和精力。周文标先生是上海市作家协会的会员，我为我们作协有这么一位孜孜不倦向世界推广中国传统文化的同仁感到骄傲。衷心祝贺他的"处世三奇书"汉英对照本成功出版，这是明清小品走向世界的一次积极尝试。期待他有更多新著在不久的将来问世。

　　10 years ago, when Mr. Zhou Wenbiao's *The Roots of Wisdom* in Chinese-English version was about to be published by Shanghai People's Publishing House, I wrote a preface for him. As I know, Mr. Zhou has been unceasingly spending most of his spare time on translating and compiling Chinese classics in English for more than ten years, and has made an active scrutiny into the modes of presentation. This time, he and Baihuazhou Literature and Art Press jointly plan to issue the "Three Canons of Personal Cultivation" in the form of three-in-one packing, which shows how much time and energy he has devoted in this respect. Mr. Zhou is a member of Shanghai Writers Association, and I am proud to have such a colleague who has been working so tirelessly to introduce Chinese traditional culture to the world. Here I'd like to extend my hearty congratulations on his successful publication of the Chinese-English

"Three Canons of Personal Cultivation", thinking that it is a positive attempt for the sketches of the Ming and Qing Dynasties to go abroad. Furthermore, I'll look forward to seeing his more new works to be published in the near future.

是为序。

It's my pleasure to write this preface as above.

2018 年 7 月 31 日于四步斋

Four-Pace Study in Shanghai
July 31st, 2018

序

Introduction to *Meditative Notes in Solitude*

周文标
Zhou Wenbiao

《小窗幽记》凡 194 则，为《处世三奇书》的第二部。

Meditative Notes in Solitude, the second book of the "Three Canons of Personal Cultivation", contains 194 sketches in all.

陈继儒（1558 年—1639 年），《小窗幽记》的作者，明末文学家、书画家，字仲醇，号眉公、麋公，华亭（今上海松江）人。诸生，年二十九，隐居小昆山，后居东佘山，杜门著述，工诗善文，书法苏、米，兼能绘事，屡受诏用，皆以疾辞。擅墨梅、山水，画梅多册页小幅，自然随意，意态萧疏。论画倡导文人画，持南北宗论，重视画家的修养，赞同书画同源，有《梅花册》《云山卷》等传世。著述除《小窗幽记》（又名《醉古堂剑扫》）外，还有《太平清话》《安得长者言》《模世语》《狂夫之言》《见闻录》《六合同春》《陈眉公诗余》《虎荟》《眉公杂著》《吴葛将军墓碑》《妮古录》等。

Chen Jiru (1558-1639), the author of this book, is a man of letters, calligrapher and painter of the Ming Dynasty, styled Zhongchun, Meigong or Migong, born in Huating (now Songjiang District, Shanghai), who,after admitted as a scholar, began his seclusion in Small Kunshan at the age of 29 and then in East Sheshan, focusing on writing. Being an adept in composing poems and essays, he laid great store on imitating Su Shi and Mi Fu in calligraphy and paintings, and declined the imperial edicts time and again on the plea of indisposition. He was good at drawing plums and mountains with black ink and habitually had his paintings of plum made into small albums brimming with natural casualness and easy grace. Theoretically, he insisted that painting should be exactly literati one no matter which school it belongs to, and that the accomplishment of a painter should be emphasized, and calligraphy and painting should be regarded as homologous. His *Album of Plum* and *Roll of Cloudy Mountain* are well known to the world. In addition to *Meditative Notes in Solitude*, he also wrote books such as *Taiping Qinghua, Ande Zhangzheyan, Mushiyu, Kuangfuzhiyan, Jianwenlu, Liuhe Tongchun, Chen Meigong Shiyu, Huhui, Meigong Zazhu, Wu Ge Jiangjun Mubei, Nigulu* and etc.

明末距今并不久远，但是有关《小窗幽记》成书的说法却不少，歧义颇多：有的说《小窗幽记》全书共 12 卷，分醒、情、峭、灵、素、景、韵、奇、绮、豪、法、倩 12 个主题；有的说《小窗幽记》全书 12 卷只轶剩 7 卷；也有的说《小窗幽记》全书 12 卷大半已轶，今仅存醒、情、峭、灵 4 卷；甚至还有人认为，《小窗幽记》系明人陆绍珩（1624 年前后尚在世）所著。这些莫衷一是的说法直接导致当今书市上出现了各种版本的《小窗幽记》。

It is not very far away from the late Ming Dynasty, but still there have existed many disputes about the formation and version of *Meditative Notes in Solitude*. Some said that there were 12 volumes in total, respectively termed as Xing (clear-headedness), Qing (love between sexes), Qiao (self-extrication), Ling (spirit), Su (simplicity), Jing (scenes), Yun (charm), Qi (splendor or excellence), Qi (prettiness), Hao (boldness or heroicness), Fa (transcending the mundane world), and Qian (beautifulness or attractiveness); some said there were only 7 volumes still extant; some said the majority of the volumes were missing, only the first four volumes were remaining; and some even thought *Meditative Notes in Solitude* was attributed to Lu Shaoheng (still alive in 1624). Such a wide spectrum of objections on this book has directly resulted in various versions nowadays.

《小窗幽记》另一个值得关注的是刊印时间问题。据史料记载，《小窗幽记》首版问世于乾隆三十五年，也即 1770 年。时有文人陈本敬作序如是：

Besides the difference of versions, the time of the book's printing is also a question worth noting. According to historical materials, *Meditative Notes in Solitude* first appeared in the thirty-fifth year of Qianlong (1770), prefaced by Chen Benjing, another man of letters of the early Qing Dynasty. The full text of the preface is as follows:

太上立德，其次立言，言者心声，而人品学术恒由此见焉。无论词躁、词俭、词烦、词支，徒蹈尚口之戒，倘语大而夸，谈理而腐，亦岂可以为训乎？然则欲求传世行远，名山不朽，必贵有以居其要矣。眉公先生负一代盛名，立志高尚，著述等身，曾集《小窗幽记》以自娱，泄天地之秘笈，撷经史之菁华，语带烟霞，韵谐金石，醒世持世，一字不落言筌。挥尘风声，直夺清谈之席；解颐语妙，常发斑管之花。所谓端庄杂流漓，尔雅兼温文，有美斯臻，无奇不备。夫岂卮言无当，徒以资覆瓿之用乎？许昌崔维东博学好古，欲付剞劂，以公同好，问序于余，因不辞谫陋，特为之弁言简端。

The best is to cultivate virtue, the next best, to establish arguments. The one who establishes arguments actually speaks his own mind, wherefrom his moral character and academic knowledge can be seen. The establishment of arguments is a matter of wording and expression, the most important thing of which lies in guarding against a loose tongue. If one regardlessly indulges in exaggeration and stubbornly clings to outworn rules and ideas, how can he inspire his fellow beings? The eternity of writings can only be realized through the words uttered to the point and capable of standing to the test of time. As a prolific writer, Mr. Meigong was in high repute all his life for his noble aspiration. He compiled *Meditative Notes in Solitude* to amuse himself by revealing the secret how to be a worthy man between heaven and earth, picking extracts from classics and history and then relating them with elegant expressions and rhyme of metal and stone to enlighten the world without falling in the net of words. His writings were superior and well esteemed among the clear-and-upright sketches. To make people understand and laugh at the same time, he often aired his exquisite opinions with witty remarks much in little. In his writing, stateliness matched with fluency, elegance accompanied by gentleness, beauty approaching perfection, nothing is too wonderful and marvelous. He knew clearly that casual utterances, if not appropriate, can only be good for nothing. Now, Cui Weidong of Xuchang, a profound scholar fond of classics and with the same taste as the author's, intends to print the book to meet the unfulfilled wish of the author and requests me to write a preface for it. Despite of my little talent and less learning, I would still like to render the short preface as this.

乾隆三十五年岁次庚寅春月，昌平陈本敬仲思氏书于聚星书院之谢青堂。

Written in the spring of the thirty-fifth year of Qianlong
By Chen Benjing of Changping
Hall of Xieqing of Star-gathering Academy

在这篇序中，作序之人除了誉美之词外，直接称谓《小窗幽记》作者为"眉公先生"，而"眉公"正是陈继儒的雅号。由于"乾隆三十五年"离作者去世中间隔了131年，有人因此说《小窗幽记》

是伪作。对此，译者并不认同，反倒以为这极有可能跟一段骇人听闻的丑恶历史有关：作者卒于明王朝行将覆灭的 1639 年，而付梓的时间却是 1770 年，这中间一百多年恰恰是清王朝连续四代皇帝大兴文字狱的时期，捕风捉影，冤杀株连，残酷程度为华夏有史以来所未见。书中第 71 则有这样的内容："料今天下皆妇人矣。封疆缩其地，而中庭之歌舞犹喧；战血枯其人，而满座貂蝉自若。我辈书生，既无诛乱讨贼之柄，而一片报国之忱，惟于寸楮尺字间见之。使天下之须眉面妇人者，亦瞿然有起色。" 陈继儒离世前在自己的书中留下这么一段呼吁抵抗清军入侵的文字，在后来清王朝统治集团的高压之下自然是见不得天日的。由此推断《小窗幽记》的刊印之路因这场文字狱而受阻，想必还是有一定依据的。今日我辈有幸捧读这么一本因幽禁而被尘封过一个多世纪的清言古籍，怎能不感慨上苍有眼，造化无欺？！

Chen Jiru died in 1639, but his book was first printed in 1770, between which there were 131 years apart. It is because of this long interval that someone held that the book was a fake. But I cannot agree and think instead that the late printing of the book is most likely to have something to do with an appalling history of ugliness caused by the first four emperors of the Qing Dynasty. Just as the history shows, since the establishment of the Qing Dynasty in 1644, the new rulers, in order to strengthen their reign, had carried out a ruthless literary inquisition of nearly a century and half against those whose writings were considered even slightest offensive by the imperial court, never seen before.

"In my opinion, today's men at court are all sissyish. They sing and dance to their hearts' content in the magnificent halls while the frontiers are being lost one after another. They have fair maids to attend their grand parties as if nothing had happened while the generals and soldiers are fighting to the last drop of their blood along the borders. We scholars, with warm hearts to serve our country, but not entitled to make war on the invaders, can only write with pens to express our deep concern for the situation, hoping that all the sissy men at court will be aroused from indifference and show up as real men."

This is the full text of No. 71 sketch picked from *Meditative*

Notes in Solitude, in which the author appealed for resistance against the Qing troops. From this we may deduce the reason why the book had been prohibited for so long a time. Today when we luckily have the book in our hands and read the content as this, how can we not felicitate ourselves with emotion on the favor Heaven has done to us!

2017 年 9 月于上海

Shanghai, China
September, 2017

目 录
Contents

14. Collecting and appreciating the calligraphies and paintings of notables are matters of elegance; but if too crazy about so doing, one will look like a merchant.

15. 轻财聚人 律己服人 /015

15. Grudge your money not and you can gather fellow beings; be strict with yourself and you can convince the public.

16. 将难放怀一放 则万境宽 /016

16. Only when you let go of the thing you are most attached to, can the world you have in sight be ever broader.

17. 大事难事看担当 逆境顺境看襟度 /017

17. To affirm if a man is reliable or not is to observe what he does when faced with important and/or difficult things.

18. 以我攻人 不如使人自露 /018

18. To let others own up to their faults is better than to censure the faulty for their wrong doings.

19. 宁为随世庸愚 勿为欺世豪杰 /019

19. Better be a mediocre person who goes with the flow than a hero who cheats the world.

20. 习忙可以销福 得谤可以销名 /020

20. Immersing yourself in your own business enables leisure and ease; being able to stand slanders wins good fame.

21. 人之嗜节 当以德消之 /021

21. The addiction of reputation had better be controlled by moral cultivation.

22. 一念之善 吉神随之 /022

22. A merciful idea in your mind makes the auspicious spirit come after you.

23. 梦里不能张主 泉下安得分明 /023

23. How can a claim unable to come into existence in dreams be clarified in the netherworld?

24. 人了了不知了 不知了了是了了 /024

24. Seemingly intelligent and perceptive are those who have no idea about being free of mundane concerns, and therefore do not know what extrication is.

25. 人我往来 是第一快活世界 /025

25. Unbiased communication between people is the most joyful thing under heaven.

26. 不必无恶邻 不必无损友 /026

26. There's no need to care too much if there are wicked ones in neighborhood or harmful friends in social contact.

27. 君子小人 五更检点 /027

27. To affirm if you are a noble man or a mean fellow, you'd better examine yourself in the early morning.

28. 以道窒欲 则心自清 /028

28. Put your desire under the control of ethical principles, and you will naturally have a pure heart.

29. 先达后近 交友道也 /029

29. First be communicative and then be friendly with, — this is the way of making friends.

30. 形骸非亲 大地亦幻 /030

30. The body we have will no longer be ours in the end; the earth is nothing but a world of illusions.

31. 寂而常惺 惺而常寂 /031

31. Be clear-headed when in quiet and be quiet when clear-headed.

32. 童子智少 少而愈完 /032

32. Children know little about the world,

so the less their knowledge the more intact their inborn nature.

33. 常思考 多检点 /033

33. Try hard to develop a habit of thinking diligently and self-reflecting frequently.

34. 脱厌如释重 带恋如担枷 /034

34. Out of poverty, the poor die content; burdened with wealth, the rich remain in fetters all their life.

35. 透得名利关 透得生死关 /035

35. Free yourself from the desire for fame and gain and penetrate the issue of life and death.

36. 多躁者 必无沉潜之识 /036

36. A man of impetuous disposition has no deep insight.

37. 佳思忽来 书能下酒 /037

37. When a good frame of mind suddenly emerges, even a book can be a dish to go with wine.

38. 生死老病 谁能透过 /038

38. Without a deep understanding of the world, who can see through the implications of life and death, old and sick?

39. 真放肆不在饮酒高歌 /039

39. To be truly free and natural, one does not have to drink and chant with wide abandon.

40. 人生待足何时足 /040

40. When will it be the time if one only stops to feel fully satisfied?

41. 云烟影里见真身 /041

41. Only amidst the shadows of clouds and mists can one see one's real self.

42. 明霞可爱 瞬眼辄空 /042

42. The bright sun rays will soon come to naught though they look lovely.

43. 不怀好意者 我自不理会 /043

43. Ignore the one who doesn't mean well.

44. 有誉于前 不若无毁于后 /044

44. Seeking praise in the presence of people is not as good as avoiding vilification from behind your back.

45. 无稽之言 是在不听听耳 /045

45. Talks with no ground to stand on are not worthwhile to take seriously even if you overheard about them.

46. 拨开才是手段 立定方见脚跟 /046

46. Eliminate the interference of vanity and hold your foot firmly in the raging wind and rain.

47. 身在事外 宜悉利害 /047

47. To comment on a matter none of your business, you should first find out all the right and wrong causes in it.

48. 谈空反被空迷 /048

48. Those who are fond of talking about phantoms are finally confused by the phantoms.

49. 贫不足羞 贱不足恶 /049

49. It's not a shame to be poor and not a disgrace to be humble.

50. 彼无望德 此无示恩 /050

50. You expect me no favor and I show you no kindness.

51. 当为情死 不当为情怨 /051

51. One can die for love but should not resent it.

52. 缩不尽相思地 补不完离恨天 /054

52. For the lovers at parting or in two places, there is bitterness unspeakable.

53. 梦醒心不归 /055

53. The dream is finished but the heart yearning for the love is still lingering in the dreamland.

54. 我幸在不痴不慧中 /056

54. I congratulate myself on being in the middle between the wise and the stupid.

55. 出相思海 下离恨天 /057

55. A merciful raft or an affectional ladder may save the separated lovers from deep lovesickness.

56. 花柳藏淑女 雨云襄王梦 /058

56. A nice lady amid flowers and willows can never be traced while rain and clouds had never attended the King.

57. 天若有情天亦老 /060

57. If the heaven had a heart as humans, how old he would be today!

58. 绝代美女 终归黄土 /061

58. Even the peerless goddesses like Xishi will become piles of soil in the end.

59. 杨柳沾啼痕 三叠唱离恨 /062

59. Grief at parting and sorrow of separation are always the eternal theme of poetry.

60. 弄柳拈花 尽是销魂之处 /063

60. Play with beautiful women, and what you gain will be no more than the soul-consuming pleasures.

61. 豆蔻不消心上恨 /065

61. The cardamom spray would not easily release her love grievance from the heart.

62. 截住巫山不放云 /066

62. Block the valleys of Mount Wu, so as not to let the clouds float away.

63. 那忍重看娃鬟绿 /067

63. A deserted fair maid is not in the mood to gaze at her own face and hair in the mirror.

64. 空闺哀怨 薄幸惊魂 /068

64. The sadness of a deserted woman often makes the fickle man ashamed for his heartlessness.

65. 良缘易合 知己难投 /069

65. A good match is easy to make while a confidant, if no longer compatible, is hard to get along.

66. 蝶憩香风 尚多芳梦 /070

66. Bathed in the fragrant wind, even an emotional butterfly will have sweet images in succession.

67. 无端饮却相思水 /071

67. A drink of acacia water and one will no longer believe that lovesickness can drive the lovers to death.

68. 多情成恋 薄命何嗟 /072

68. Amorous people tend to fall in love with the opposite sex, but some women would sigh with sorrow when ill-fated.

69. 清风好伴 明月故人 /073

69. A gust of fresh breeze can be a good companion and an old friend, the emitting moon.

70. 平生云水心 春花秋月语 /074

70. To a person who adores the beauty of nature, autumn moon and spring flowers are always the only subject.

71. 封疆缩地 中庭歌舞犹喧 /075

71. The sissy men at court sing and dance to their hearts' content while the frontiers are in decline.

72. 士不晓廉耻 衣冠狗彘 /076

72. Scholar-knights who have no sense of shame and dignity are only dogs and pigs in hat and clothes.

73. 宁以风霜自挟　毋为鱼鸟亲人 /077

73. The man of integrity would rather go through all the hardships on their own than act as the pooled fish or caged bird totally dependent on human beings for living.

74. 仕夫贪财好货　乃有爵之乞丐 /078

74. A high-ranking official, if merely interested in seeking material gains, is a beggar with title of nobility.

75. 一失足成千古恨 /079

75. A false slip may cause a lifelong regret.

76. 圣贤不白之衷　托之日月 /080

76. Aspirations unable to be expressed by the sages can be entrusted to the sun and moon to declare.

77. 士大夫爱钱　书香化为铜臭 /081

77. When a scholar turns his attention to money, the fragrance of books will become stink of copper coin.

78. 心为形役　尘世马牛 /082

78. Allow your body to labor your mind, and you will be the same as horse or cattle in life.

79. 留有余智　提防不测 /083

79. Give no full play to your wisdom in order to save some strength to deal with possible unexpected occurrences.

80. 做事要担当　又要善摆脱 /084

80. In dealing with the world's affairs, one should know when and how to advance and retreat.

81. 假认不得真　巧藏不得拙 /085

81. What is false cannot be true; whoever is clever cannot hide his clumsiness.

82. 量晴较雨　弄月嘲风 /086

82. It's quite a thing to detect the climatic change or invite friends of yours to enjoy with you the moon and breeze.

83. 放下仙佛心　方名为得道 /087

83. Expel the desire for being an immortal-like Buddha, and you will comprehend what the Way is.

84. 执拗者福轻　圆融者禄厚 /088

84. Pigheaded persons have inadequate good fortune while those of mellow character receive affluent emolument.

85. 达人撒手悬崖 /089

85. A man well versed in the way of life is he that knows when to rein in at the brink of a precipice.

86. 身世浮名余以梦蝶视之 /090

86. One'd better look at fame and glory with an illusive vision rather than the naked eyes.

87. 百折不回　方能百变不穷 /091

87. Only with a firm will can one find out a foolproof way to deal with various unexpected occurrences.

88. 立业建功　实地着脚 /092

88. Be earnest and down-to-earth if you are determined to establish a competency and make a contribution.

89. 兢兢业业心思　潇潇洒洒趣味 /093

89. A man devoted to scholarship should not only have assiduous thoughts in study but also elegant tastes for life.

90. 无事提防　有事镇定 /094

90. Be on alert when nothing has happened and when something has happened, be calm and collected.

91. 穷通之境未遭 主持之局已定 /095

91. Plan the layout of personal development prior to the coming of tough time or prosperity.

92. 枝头秋叶 檐前野鸟 /096

92. Not be the autumn leaves hanging on the branches or the caged birds under the eaves.

93. 刚强终不胜柔弱 /097

93. The hard are no match for the supple in the end.

94. 声应气求之夫 风行水上之文 /098

94. Good friendship depends on mutual understandings; good writings are like the wind skimming over the water.

95. 才智英敏者 宜以学问摄其躁 /099

95. The man of ability and intelligence should harmonize his impetuous disposition with acquired knowledge.

96. 身居轩冕之中 须有山林气味 /100

96. Those who enjoy high positions and handsome salaries should not be dispensed of the plain makings of a hermit.

97. 少言语以当贵 多著述以当富 /101

97. Take it as acquiring dignity to speak less and as gaining wealth to write aplenty.

98. 要做男子 须负刚肠 /102

98. One who wants to be a real man should be of iron-will and stoneheartedness.

99. 柔玉温香 可成白骨 /103

99. Women, even with jade-like skin and fragrant flesh, will finally become white bones.

100. 空烦恼场 绝营求念 /104

100. Banish the vexing thoughts, abandon the desire for fame and gain, and you will enjoy ease and liberty.

101. 闲随老衲清谭 戏与骚人白战 /105

101. When not occupied, it's quite a joy to chat with an old monk and a fun to chant with a poet.

102. 宁为真士夫 不为假道学 /106

102. Rather be an honest Confucian scholar than a sanctimonious Taoist follower.

103. 觑破兴衰究竟 人我得失冰消 /107

103. A perception of the outcomes in rise and fall helps people to give up their thoughts to personal gains and losses.

104. 名山乏侣 不解壁上芒鞋 /108

104. Outing to a mountainous resort with no good company coming along is not as desirable as staying at home.

105. 无技最苦 多技最劳 /109

105. Those with no skill are most hardworking and utterly exhausted, those with multiple skills.

106. 才士不妨泛驾 诤臣岂合模棱 /110

106. A man of talent may well roam the world at will, but a court official in submitting admonitions is not allowed to speak in an equivocal way.

107. 宁为薄幸狂夫 不作厚颜君子 /111

107. Rather be a frivolous maniac than a shameless hypocrite.

108. 魑魅满前 笑著阮家无鬼论 /112

108. When everywhere are seen the ones who appear as sinister as the ghosts, I can't help pouring ridicule

on the viewpoint of non-existence of ghosts.

109. 至音不合众　至宝不同众好 /114

109. Music played to its extreme is hard for all to appreciate; treasures of the supreme class are difficult for all to appraise.

110. 世人白昼寐语 /116

110. People love to repeat at daytime what they talked about in dreams.

111. 拨开世上尘氛　消却心中鄙吝 /117

111. Turn away the turmoil and confusion from without and expel the sordidness and stinginess from within.

112. 才子安心草舍　佳人适意蓬门 /118

112. A talented scholar is he who is willing to reside in a thatched hut; a virtuous beauty is she who is content to be the daughter-in-law of a humble family.

113. 喜传语者　不可与语 /119

113. Do not speak your mind to those who are keenly fond of gossip.

114. 不留昨日之非　不执今日之是 /120

114. What was wrong yesterday should not be retained; what is correct today may not be held too fast.

115. 炫奇之疾　医以平易 /121

115. To be unassuming and amiable is a remedy for the flaw in resorting to novelty.

116. 人常想病时　则尘心便减 /122

116. Frequently reflect on the hard time of being ill, and one will moderate his desire for material gains.

117. 恩爱吾之仇也 /123

117. The affair of man and woman is my enemy.

118. 人生善读书　享世间清福 /124

118. The person who has books and time to read enjoys leisurely happiness in life.

119. 古人不掩瑕瑜　今人难知真伪 /125

119. The ancients never concealed their defects while the moderns are like antiques you can never tell real from false.

120. 以忍制己情　以恕制人情 /126

120. Restrain the desires of our own and tolerate the inveterate habits of others.

121. 随遇而安　何不清闲 /127

121. A leisurely life will be assured if one can adapt himself to the circumstances.

122. 浮云有常情　流水多浓旨 /128

122. Floating clouds are more understandable than human affairs and running waters more affectionate than human feelings.

123. 贫士肯济人　闹场能笃学 /129

123. A poor scholar who is ready to lend a helping hand can concentrate on study in the hubbub.

124. 了心自了事　逃世应逃名 /130

124. To eliminate a concern is to bring an end to the thing concerned; to renounce the world is to expel the desire for fame from within.

125. 风流得意　鬼胜顽仙 /131

125. An unconventional talented ghost prevails over a stubborn immortal.

126. 不因人言而悟　不因外境而得 /132

126. Realization obtained through others' reminding and interest aroused by exterior causes are always not constant.

127. 简淡出豪杰 忠孝成神仙 /133

127. To be a hero, one should start with ordinariness; to be a deity, one should start with loyalty and filialness.

128. 浇花种树 道人魔障 /134

128. The hobby to water flowers and plant trees is at last a barrier in the heart set by a monster.

129. 天下之灵 千古如新 /135

129. The spirit of the world will remain as ever fresh as it has been.

130. 人生有三乐 阅经会友云游 /136

130. Reading Buddhist scriptures, entertaining friends and outing to roam the world are the three great pleasures in life.

131. 眼里无点灰尘 方可读书千卷 /137

131. Only by keeping your eyes away from dust can you read a thousand books as you will.

132. 不作风波于世上 /138

132. One won't be worried if one does nothing to trouble the world.

133. 无事不乐而忧 是一座活地狱 /139

133. Worrying while nothing has happened makes people live in hell.

134. 必出世者 方能入世 /140

134. Before traveling in the mundane world one must first make up his mind to transcend it.

135. 人有一字不识而多诗意 /141

135. There are people who can't read a word and yet can give utterances full of poetic flavor.

136. 眉上几分愁 且去观棋酌酒 /142

136. When you are in bad mood, go and watch a chess game, or go and have a sip.

137. 得心上本来 方可言了心 /143

137. Only when recognizing the character of one's own nature can one understand the essence of one's own heart.

138. 调性谱情 功在其法 /144

138. To adjust your temperament and adapt yourself to the circumstances well depend on the methods to apply.

139. 好茶涤烦 好酒消忧 /145

139. A good tea can get rid of vexed thoughts while a good wine can dissolve the gloom in the heart.

140. 破除烦恼木鱼声 见澈性灵优钵影 /146

140. To get rid of worries, go and listen to the sound of wooden clappers; to penetrate the human nature, go and have a look at the green lotus.

141. 太闲生恶业 太清类俗情 /147

141. Too leisurely a life makes one loose in behavior; too self-contained a deed begets poor taste.

142. 灵丹一粒 点化俗情 /148

142. A pure and clear mind helps to get rid of vulgarity.

143. 妖冶成泉下骷髅 功名是梦中蝴蝶 /149

143. Beauty can never last and merits are illusive.

144. 独坐禅房 意揖达摩 /150

144. Sit alone in the Buddhist abode to gaze at *The Budhidharma Facing to the Wall Painting*.

145. 以正敛放 以趣通板 /152

145. Restrain yourself with uprightness and release yourself with interest.

146. 疑善信恶 满腔杀机 /153

146. Suspect when aware of philanthropic act and believe when told

of wrongdoings, — these are the signs of a dark psychology.

147. 能脱俗便是奇 不合污便是清 /154

147. Rising above vulgarity is out of the ordinary; never associating with evil elements is unsullied.

148. 君子尽心利济 即此便是立命 /155

148. A gentleman establishes his worth and estate by helping others wholeheartedly.

149. 读史耐讹字 闲居耐俗汉 /156

149. To read historical books one has to endure the misspelling words; to live a leisurely life one has to endure the mean fellows.

150. 声色娱情 何若净几明窗 /157

150. Seeking pleasures in sensual entertainment is not as good as living a clean, tidy life in peace and ease.

151. 心上无事好快活 何必情欲乃为乐 /158

151. Enjoy yourself while you may, and you will be happy right off. Why take love affairs as the sole happiness!

152. 兴来醉倒 机息忘怀 /159

152. Drink till drunk when your spirits run high; forget the plots and schemes to keep your heart at ease.

153. 烦恼之场 何种不有 /160

153. In the fair of vexations, there are various vexations.

154. 休便休去 了时无了 /161

154. Rest while you may, or you will have no time to do so even if you want to.

155. 意亦甚适 梦亦同趣 /162

155. Even in their dreams the good companions are also temperamentally compatible.

156. 业净成慧眼 无物到茅庵 /163

156. Remove the sinful intents, and you will gain insight; banish the material desires, and you will refine yourself even in a thatched hut.

157. 犬吠鸡鸣 恍似云中世界 /164

157. By listening to the dogs' barking and cocks' crowing, one will feel as if roaming in a cloudy wonderland.

158. 异士未必在山泽 /165

158. The eccentric persons may not dwell in the place among the mountains and rivers.

159. 可爱之人可怜 可恶之人可惜 /166

159. All the darlings are worthy to be cherished; all the hatefuls only deserve to be regretted.

160. 急之不白 操之不从 /167

160. There are things one cannot make clear in a hurry and persons who cannot follow what is instructed.

161. 比上不足 比下有余 /168

161. Worse off than some, better off than many.

162. 俭为贤德 贫是美称 /169

162. To be willing to live a frugal life is a good virtue; to be content with poverty is a good fame.

163. 唤醒梦中之梦 窥见身外之身 /170

163. Wake up from a fancy and stay sober, and one will perceive the essence of human nature.

164. 打透生死关 参破名利场 /171

164. See through the causes of life and death and penetrate the vanity of fame and wealth.

165. 一笔写出 便是作手 /172

165. A good poet can finish in one

breath a poem depicting the landscape before the eye and the appeal in the heart.

166. 隐逸林中无荣辱 /173

166. A man who lives as a hermit gives no thought to the personal honor and disgrace.

167. 皮囊速坏 神识常存 /174

167. Human bodies are easy to decay while the power of human intelligence will ever exist.

168. 闻谤勿怒 见誉勿喜 /175

168. Don't be angry when slandered, nor be complacent when adulated.

169. 人胜我无害 我胜人非福 /176

169. To me, it's neither a hurt if somebody else is one-up on me, nor a blessing if I one-upman somebody else.

170. 闭门是深山 读书有净土 /177

170. To take a self-reflection, there is no need to go into the mountains; to read books, no need to find a quiet place.

171. 欲见圣人气象 必须胸中洁净 /178

171. To see the dignified bearing of a sage, one should first make his own heart pure and clear.

172. 成名每在穷苦日 /179

172. It often follows that one makes a name for himself when caught in dire straits.

173. 让利精于取利 /180

173. Surrendering some profits deserved is cleverer than keeping them.

174. 求福速祸 泰然得福 /181

174. Calm manner in crisis turns bad fortune into good.

175. 看书不可拘泥旧说 /182

175. In reading a book, one should not confine himself to the existing theories.

176. 但识琴中趣 何劳弦上音 /183

176. If you can tell the entertainment in the lute, is there a need to labor your fingers over the strings?

177. 出一言解之 是无量功德 /184

177. It's an immeasurable merit to forward a suggestion to see others through their difficulties.

178. 伶人代古人 似今人为文 /185

178. The actors and actresses play the ancients in the way the modern writers create their writings.

179. 闲有余日 正可学问 /186

179. Unoccupied times are the right opportunity for learning and consultation.

180. 简傲不可谓高 阿谀不可谓谦 /187

180. Acting with arrogance cannot be regarded as dignity; licking others' boots cannot be regarded as modesty.

181. 丹青乃无言之诗 诗句乃有言之画 /188

181. Painting is speechless poetry, poetry is a talking painting.

182. 云霞为侣伴 青松为心知 /189

182. The floating clouds are my companion and the green pines my confidant.

183. 耳目宽则天地窄 /190

183. Too many desires of the ears and eyes make the heaven and earth narrow.

184. 江水汩汩 疑有湘灵 /191

184. The murmuring stream raises one

up to believe that there are goddesses in the water picking the strings.

185. 有书癖而无剪裁 徒号书橱 /192

185. One who has a hobby to collect books but does not know how to make a professional selection is only a bookcase.

186. 鸟啼花落 有会于心 /193

186. The crying of birds and the falling of flowers are pleasant to a knowing heart.

187. 山峦之胜 妙于天成 /194

187. The attraction of a mountain is mostly brought forth by Nature.

188. 清闲无事 坐卧随心 /195

188. Those unoccupied and having nothing to do are enabled to sit or sleep at will.

189. 舞蝶游蜂 落花飞絮 /196

189. Full of imagination are the dancing butterflies and roaming bees as well as the fallen petals and flying catkins.

190. 鸟栖高枝 士隐岩穴 /197

190. Birds like to perch on high branches while hermits prefer to dwell in the cave.

191. 混迹尘中 高视物外 /198

191. See beyond the material world while going through its hubbub.

192. 五夜鸡鸣 一觉睡醒 /199

192. The crows of a cock early in the morning wake me up from a deep sleep.

193. 取凉于扇 汲水于井 /200

193. A fan fetches cool; well water quenches thirst.

194. 飞凌缥缈 坐看氤氲 /201

194. Set your mind in the world of illusions by sitting yourself to watch the mists, gathering and dispersing.

1. 安得一服清凉散 人人解醒

1. Where to find a medication to draw the intoxicated ones back to a clear-headed state?

食中山之酒①，一醉千日，今之昏昏逐逐②，无一日不醉。趋名者醉于朝③，趋利者醉于野④，豪者⑤醉于声色车马。安得一服清凉散，人人解醒⑥?

【中文注释】 ① 中山之酒: 一种据说是中山人狄希酿造的、能让人一饮醉千日的烈酒。
② 昏昏逐逐: 昏昏沉沉, 不可终日。
③ 朝: 朝廷。隐喻官场。
④ 野: 原意指与 "朝廷" 相对的 "民间"。此处借喻跟利益相关的 "生意场"。
⑤ 豪者: 整天花天酒地、纵情享乐的人。
⑥ 解醒: 醒, 醉酒状。解醒。即解酒或醒酒之意。

【今文解译】 清醒的人喝了中山烈酒, 就会一醉不起, 千日不醒。而今天的人们尽管滴酒不沾, 却也似喝醉了酒一般, 整日里沉醉于对声色名利的追逐之中: 好名的沉醉于升官加爵, 好利的沉醉于敛财致富, 好纵情享乐的沉醉于花天酒地。哪里能找到使人清醒的良药, 拯救这些沉醉中的人们?

【English Translation】

It was told that a sip of the strong liquid brewed by the master of Zhongshan Mountain could make a clear-headed one lost in drunkenness for a thousand days. But people of present day, though without drinking a drop of wine, are all too intoxicated to be themselves each and every day: those longing for fame and rank are so intoxicated with the court; those striving for economic profit are so intoxicated with the fair; and those engaged in extravagance are so intoxicated with luxury and sensuality. O where to find a medication to act as the dose of sobriety to dispel the intoxications and draw the intoxicated ones back to a clear-headed state!

2. 澹泊之守　镇定之操

2. It's good to foster the integrity of seeking no fame and wealth and cultivate the ability of keeping calm and collected.

澹泊之守^①，须从浓艳场^②中试^③来；镇定之操^④，还向纷纭境^⑤上勘^⑥过。

【中文注释】　① 守：操守；志节；名节。
② 浓艳场：弥漫骄奢淫逸气氛的场所。此处喻名利场。
③ 试：测试。
④ 操：本意也是操守，此处可理解为能耐、潜质、素质等。
⑤ 纷纭境：纷乱复杂的环境。
⑥ 勘：检验；验证。

【今文解译】　一个人是否有淡泊名利的志节，一定要经名利场的诱惑考验方能知晓。
一个人是否有临事镇定的素质，还必须在纷乱复杂的环境里加以验证。

【English Translation】

The integrity of seeking no fame and wealth is fostered and tested in a place where riches and honor prevail.
The ability to be perfectly calm and collected is cultivated and verified in a great diversity of chaos and confusions.

3. 市恩不如报德　要誉不如逃名

3. Anticipating return is no better than repaying kindness; asking for glory is no better than eluding fame.

市恩①不如报德之为厚，要誉不如逃名之为适，矫情不如直节之为真。

【中文注释】　　① 市恩：市，交易；买卖；有所图。市恩意指为求得某种利益或回报而施恩于人。

【今文解译】　　施恩图报不如以德报恩来得厚道。
索要荣誉不如回避名声来得适宜。
做事矫情不如为人直率来得实诚。

【 English Translation 】

To anticipate return while doing good is not as good as to requite others' kindness with gratitude.

To ask for glory is not as desirable as to elude fame.

To be pretentious is not as earnest as to be forthright.

4. 使人有面前之誉　不若无背后之毁

4. To make people praise you right in your face is no better than not to make them vilify you behind your back.

　　使人有面前之誉，不若使人无背后之毁；使人有乍交之欢，不若使人无久处之厌。

【今文解译】　与其让人当着你的面夸赞你，不如不让人在你的背后指指点点。
　　　　　　　与其让人一见面就对你产生好感，不如不让人因处久而嫌厌你。

【English Translation】

To make people praise you right in your face is no better than not to make them vilify you behind your back.

To make people show a liking to you at first meeting is no better than not to make them think scorn of you in the course of time.

5. 天薄我福　吾厚吾德

5. Should Heaven make my fortune inadequate, I would increase the store of my virtue to replenish it.

　　天薄我福，吾厚吾德以迎之；天劳我形，吾逸吾心以补之；天厄我遇，吾亨吾道以通之。

【今文解译】　　上天赐我的福祉不多，我就行善积德以求福报。
　　　　　　　　上天要使我辛苦劳累，我就放松身心以求弥补。
　　　　　　　　上天要让我命途坎坷，我就增强修为以求通达。

【English Translation】

Should Heaven make my fortune inadequate, I would increase the store of my virtue to replenish it.
Should Heaven labor my body too hard, I would relax my mind to reinforce it.
Should Heaven make my way obstructed, I would enhance my moral cultivation to smooth it.

6. 澹泊之士　必为浓艳者所疑

6. A man despising fame and wealth may arouse the suspicion of those who love them.

　　澹泊之士，必为浓艳者所疑；检饰之人，必为放肆者所忌。事穷势蹙之人，当原其初心；功成行满之士，要观其末路。

【今文解译】　淡泊名利的人必然会被热衷名利的人所猜疑。

为人谨慎的人往往会被肆无忌惮的人所刁难。

当一个人事业受挫、处境落魄时，我们应当看他开始做事时的初心究竟是怎样的。

当一个人事业有成、功德圆满时，我们应当观察他能否将这势头一直保持到最后。

【English Translation】

It always follows that a man despising fame and wealth should arouse the suspicion of those who love them.

It is more than common that a man discreet in word and deed should incur the jealousy of those who are reckless and unbridled.

To judge a man who has suffered failure and is now down and out, it is better to look into his original intent at the outset.

To comment on a man who has come to a successful issue, it is better to examine if he can carry his exploits to the end.

7. 好丑两得其平　贤愚共受其益

7. Let beauty and ugliness get along with one another and the wise and the stupid be favored with no discrimination.

好丑心太明，则物不契①；贤愚心太明，则人不亲②。须是内精明而外浑厚，使好丑两得其平，贤愚共受其益，才是生成的德量。

【中文注释】　① 契：契合；和睦。
② 亲：融洽；亲和；友善。

【今文解译】　美和丑分得太清楚，事物与事物就难以相互融合；聪明和愚笨分得太清楚，人与人之间就无法和睦相处。最好能做到内里精明、外表敦厚，使美的和丑的都能和平相处，聪明的和愚笨的都能从中受益，这才是包容兼蓄的道德涵养和气度。

【English Translation】

The harmony of things cannot be reached if we unduly distinguish them with beauty and ugliness. The intimacy of interpersonal relationship cannot be brought about if we overly discriminate between the wise and the stupid. In order to make the beauty and ugliness get along peacefully with one another and favor both of the wise and the stupid with no discrimination, we must keep inwardly an astute mind and outwardly an honest appearance, and thus bring the great merit of generosity to fruition.

8. 多情必至寡情　任性终不失性

8. A sentimental person is liable to become cold-hearted while a capricious fellow is hard to change his nature.

情最难久，故多情人必至寡情；性自有常，故任性人终不失性。

【今文解译】　　情爱是最难长久的，所以多情的人往往会变得寡情薄意。
　　　　　　　　天性是与生俱来的，所以任性的人不会改变自己的天性。

【English Translation】

Man's passions cannot last long, so those full of tender feelings and affections are liable to become cold-hearted.

Man's nature is innate and constant, so those with a wayward disposition will never change their nature indiscreetly.

9. 立名为贪　用术为拙

9. The person who seeks reputation for himself is called greedy; the person who resorts to craft is called clumsy.

真廉无名，立名者所以为贪；大巧无术，用术者所以为拙。

【今文解译】　真正的廉洁不需廉洁为其名：为自己树立廉洁的名声，其实就是一种贪图名声的行为。

真正的才智不需机巧为其术：靠玩弄机巧来施展才智，其实就是为了掩饰自己的笨拙。

【English Translation】

True honesty has no reputation to seek; the person who seeks reputation for himself is called greedy.

Great wisdom needs no craft to resort to; the person who resorts to craft is called clumsy.

10. 淡名利者　未忘名利之情

10. He who is disgusted at the talk about fame and wealth has not necessarily banished the desire for fame and wealth.

　　谭山林之乐①者，未必真得山林之趣；厌②名利之谭者，未必尽忘名利之情③。

【中文注释】　　① 山林之乐：指隐居山林的乐趣，与后面的"山林之趣"同义。
　　　　　　　　② 厌：厌恶；不屑。
　　　　　　　　③ 名利之情：追逐名利的欲望。

【今文解译】　　动辄谈论山林之乐的人，未必真的知道山林之乐的妙趣。
　　　　　　　　口口声声说厌恶名利的人，未必都已经抛却了名利之心。

【English Translation】

It does not necessarily follow that he who is fond of talking about the delight in living amid the mountains and forest really understands the bliss of such a life. Neither does it so that he who declares himself to be disgusted at the talk about fame and wealth has completely banished from his mind the desire for fame and wealth.

11. 伏久者　飞必高

11. The longer the bird rests in concealment, the higher it flies.

伏久者，飞必高；开先者，谢独早。

【今文解译】　鸟蛰伏久了，展翅就一飞冲天。
花开得越早，凋谢得也就越早。

【English Translation】

The longer the bird rests in concealment, the higher it flies.
The earlier the flower blooms, the sooner it fades.

12. 天欲祸人　必先以微福骄之

12. Before making one suffer, Heaven would always bestow some scanty favors on him to provoke his conceit.

　　天欲祸人，必先以微福骄^①之，要看他会受^②。天欲福人，必先以微祸儆^③之，要看他会救^④。

【中文注释】　① 骄：骄纵；纵容。
　　　　　　　② 受：承受；经受。
　　　　　　　③ 儆：警示；警告。同"警"。
　　　　　　　④ 救：救赎。此处指自我救赎。

【今文解译】　上天要降祸于一个人，一定会先给他点薄福以骄纵他，看他是否能把持自己。
　　　　　　　上天要降福于一个人，一定会先让他吃点苦以示儆诚，看他是否能自我救赎。

【English Translation】

Before making someone suffer, Heaven would habitually bestow some scanty favors on him to provoke his conceit, so as to see if he can handle or not.
Before granting favors to someone, Heaven would habitually let him suffer a little to give warning, so as to see if he can rescue himself or not.

13. 世人破绽处　多从周旋处见

13. The bad habits people have are usually detected in their social intercourses.

　　世人破绽处①，多从周旋处②见；指摘处③，多从爱护处④见；艰难处⑤，多从贪恋处⑥见。

【中文注释】　① 破绽处：此处喻缺点、缺陷或不足等。
　　　　　　　② 周旋处：此处喻待人接物，交际应酬。
　　　　　　　③ 指摘处：此处喻责备、批评或教训等。
　　　　　　　④ 爱护处：此处喻彼此关心爱护的人们。
　　　　　　　⑤ 艰难处：此处喻难以割舍的东西。
　　　　　　　⑥ 贪恋处：此处喻喜欢且不忍释手的事物。

【今文解译】　世人行为举止上的缺陷，大多出现在待人接物中；斥责或指摘，大多出于亲友间的相互关心爱护；难以割舍，大多是因为贪恋而不忍放手。

【English Translation】

So far as people at large are concerned, the faults they have are usually detected in their social intercourses; the terms of reproach against their faults are often heard among those who care for them; the objects difficult for them to give up are normally seen in the things they are crazy about.

14. 书画是雅事　贪痴亦商贾

14. Collecting and appreciating the calligraphies and paintings of notables are matters of elegance; but if too crazy about so doing, one will look like a merchant.

　　山栖是胜事，稍一萦恋①，则亦市朝②；书画赏鉴是雅事，稍一贪痴，则亦商贾；诗酒是乐事，稍一曲人，则亦地狱；好客是豁达事，稍一为俗子所扰，则亦苦海③。

【中文注释】　① 萦恋：迷恋。此处意为流连忘返。
　　　　　　　② 市朝：集市与朝廷。
　　　　　　　③ 苦海：此处含倒胃口之意。

【今文解译】　短栖山林是美事，但倘若迷上那儿不走了，山林也就成市井朝廷了。
　　　　　　　赏鉴书画是兴味雅事，但倘若沉溺其中，雅事也就成商家的买卖了。
　　　　　　　作诗饮酒是乐事，但倘若强劝而使人为之，乐事也就如同下地狱了。
　　　　　　　好客是大方之举，但倘若稍有庸俗的人掺和进来，事情也就变味了。

【English Translation】

Sojourning in the mountains is a joyful thing; but if one is too enchanted with it, the mountains will turn into marketplace or imperial court.

Collecting and appreciating the calligraphies and paintings of notables are matters of elegance; but if too crazy about so doing, one will look like a merchant.

Verse-composing and wine-drinking are pleasant things; but if done against the will of others, they will soon serve like a hell.

Being hospitable is a generous act; but if slightly disturbed by a vulgarian, the felt warm atmosphere will become disgusting.

15. 轻财聚人 律己服人

15. Grudge your money not and you can gather fellow beings; be strict with yourself and you can convince the public.

轻财足以聚人，律己足以服人，量宽足以得人，身先足以率人。

【今文解译】　不吝钱财才足以聚集人脉。
严于律己才足以使人信服。
宽宏大量才足以赢得人心。
身先士卒才足以为人表率。

【English Translation】

Grudge your money not, and you can gather fellow human beings together.
Be strict with yourself, and you can gain the power of influence.
Be lenient to others, and you can win the support from them.
Go at the head of masses, and you can be the leader of them.

16. 将难放怀一放　则万境宽

16. Only when you let go of the thing you are most attached to, can the world you have in sight be ever broader.

从极迷处识迷，则到处醒；将难放怀一放，则万境宽。

【今文解译】　将最难识破的迷局识破，那么所到之处就都能保持清醒的头脑。

将最难放下的人和事都放下，那么眼前所见的一切就都会豁然开朗。

【English Translation】

Only when you penetrate the puzzle most difficult to penetrate, can you be clear-headed wherever you go.

Only when you let go of the thing you are most attached to, can the world you have in sight be ever broader.

17. 大事难事看担当　逆境顺境看襟度

17. To affirm if a man is reliable or not is to observe what he does when faced with important and/or difficult things.

　　大事难事看担当，逆境顺境看襟度，临喜临怒看涵养，群行群止看识见。

【今文解译】　　一个人是否有担当，就看他在大事难事面前怎么去做。

一个人是否有胸襟，就看他在顺境和逆境中如何表现。

一个人是否有涵养，就看他在喜怒哀乐时的情感表达。

一个人是否有识见，就看他与众人相处时的行为举止。

【English Translation】

To make sure if a man is reliable or not is to observe what he does when confronted with important and/or difficult things.

To make sure if a man is large-minded or not is to observe how he behaves in advantage as well as in disadvantage.

To make sure if a man is well cultured or not is to observe what he acts in the face of occurrences, pleasing or annoying.

To make sure if a man is wide in experience or not is to observe how he has a go in getting along with the multitude.

18. 以我攻人 不如使人自露

18. To let others own up to their faults is better than to censure the faulty for their wrong doings.

良心在夜气清明之候，真情在箪食豆羹之间。故以我索人，不如使人自反；以我攻人，不如使人自露。

【今文解译】 一如良心发现于深夜的清醒时刻，真情流露于解人饥渴的粗茶淡饭。与其我去要求别人怎么做，不如让他们反躬自省；与其我去抨击别人的不是，不如让他们自己承认错误。

【English Translation】

Just as a good conscience is discovered in the sobriety of night, so true feelings are perceived the moment a simple meal or a plain tea is served. That's why we say that to make others willingly conduct self-examination is better than to simply instruct them how to behave themselves, and to let others own up to their faults is better than to censure the faulty for their wrong doings.

19. 宁为随世庸愚　勿为欺世豪杰

19. Better be a mediocre person who goes with the flow than a hero who cheats the world.

宁为随世之庸愚，勿为欺世之豪杰。

【今文解译】　宁做随波逐流的庸碌之辈，也不做欺世盗名的英雄豪杰。

【English Translation】

Rather be a mediocre individual who only goes with the flow than a heroic man who wins popularity by cheating the public.

20. 习忙可以销福　得谤可以销名

20. Immersing yourself in your own business enables leisure and ease; being able to stand slanders wins good fame.

　　清福上帝所吝，而习忙可以销福；清名①上帝所忌，而得谤②可以销名。

【中文注释】　① 清名：良好的名声。
　　　　　　　② 得谤：承受外来的诽谤或质疑。

【今文解译】　上帝是不会赐人以清闲生活的，但谁若有幸得到这样的生活，不妨可以使自己忙碌一点，以抵消些自己为人所嫉的成分。
　　　　　　　上帝是不会赐人以良好名声的，但谁若有幸得到这样的名声，不妨坦然面对外界的诽谤，以去掉些其实难副的东西。

【English Translation】

Life of leisure and ease is never the bliss God is to bestow. But he who happens to have got it may as well make the best of it by immersing himself in his own business.

Good reputation, if not rightly accorded, is what God despises. But he who has attained it by chance may as well live up to it by going through all the possible slanders.

21. 人之嗜节　当以德消之

21. The addiction of reputation had better be controlled by moral cultivation.

人之嗜节①，嗜文章②，嗜游侠③，如好酒然，易动客气④，当以德消之。

【中文注释】　① 节：意指名声、荣誉等。
② 文章：此处系指文学作品或者文艺。
③ 游侠：仗义，好打抱不平。
④ 易动客气：易动肝火，做事不冷静。

【今文解译】　人们像爱好美酒一样爱好名节，爱好文章，爱好侠义，做事容易冲动，所以要用道德修养来加以克制。

【English Translation】

People who like reputation and integrity, articles and chivalry as they like good wine are liable to act on impulse. Why not control the impulse by improving their inner power?

22. 一念之善　吉神随之

22. A merciful idea in your mind makes the auspicious spirit come after you.

一念之善，吉神随之；一念之恶，厉鬼随之。知此可以役使鬼神。

【今文解译】　脑子里存有善念，吉神就会伴你左右；脑子里存有恶念，恶鬼就会随你而行。明白这一点便可以让各路鬼神都乖乖地听命于你。

【English Translation】

Whenever there appears a merciful idea in your mind, the auspicious spirit will come after you. Likewise, whenever there appears a vicious idea in your mind, the evil spirit will attend you. Aware of this, you may have all the spirits, auspicious or evil, at your command.

23. 梦里不能张主　泉下安得分明

23. How can a claim unable to come into existence in dreams be clarified in the netherworld?

眉睫才交^①，梦里便不能张主^②；眼光落地^③，泉下^④又安得分明？

【中文注释】　① 眉睫才交：双眼闭合，即睡觉状。

② 张主：阐述主张。

③ 眼光落地：指垂死之人的目光。典自宋代洪迈的《夷坚支志甲·巴东太守》："盖将亡时精神消散，所谓眼光落地者此欤？"以及朱熹的《答吕子约书》之七："魄之降乎土，犹今人言眼光落地云尔。"

④ 泉下：黄泉之下，也即去世。

【今文解译】　双目闭合，安然入睡，谁也不能在梦中阐述醒时的主张。眼皮耷拉着的将亡之人，即使未入阴间又能看清什么呢？

【English Translation】

Tossing in the land of dream with the eyes fully closed, no one can enunciate what he thinks about while awake.

How can a dying person see with drooping eyelids, even if not yet settled in the netherworld?

24. 人了了不知了　不知了了是了了

24. Seemingly intelligent and perceptive are those who have no idea about being free of mundane concerns, and therefore do not know what extrication is.

佛只是个了仙，也是个了圣。人了了不知了，不知了了是了了；若知了了，便不了。

【今文解译】　佛只是个了却了尘缘的神仙，也是个摆脱了一切烦恼的圣人。貌似聪明的人不知道该了却心里的烦恼，所以不明白只有了却了心里的烦恼才是真正的聪明。如果心里还有想了却烦恼的念头，那便是还有烦恼尚未了却。

【English Translation】

Buddha is but an immortal free of mundane concerns, and also a saint that has extricated himself from the way of the world. Whoever is seemingly intelligent and perceptive has no idea about being free of mundane concerns, and therefore does not know that one who has extricated oneself from the way of the world is really intelligent and perceptive. Any attempt to seek the freedom and extrication indicates the absence of the said.

25. 人我往来 是第一快活世界

25. Unbiased communication between people is the most joyful thing under heaven.

剖去胸中荆棘以便人我往来，是天下第一快活世界。

【今文解译】 摒弃心里的不良成见，胸怀坦荡地与人们进行交往。——此乃天下第一快事！

【English Translation】

Open your mind and get rid of all the ill feelings thereof, so that the world and your self can communicate fluently with no obstruction. Isn't it the most joyful thing under heaven!

26. 不必无恶邻　不必无损友

26. There's no need to care too much if there are wicked ones in neighborhood or harmful friends in social contact.

居不必无恶邻^①，会不必无损友^②，惟在自持者两得之。

【中文注释】　① 恶邻：专事凶横霸道、无事生非、寻衅凌辱的坏邻居。

② 损友：对自己有害的朋友；对自己的品行产生不良影响的朋友。与"益友"相对。语自《论语·季氏篇》的"益者三友，损者三友：友直、友谅、友多闻，益矣；友便辟、友善柔、友便佞，损矣"。

【今文解译】　选择居住地不必非要没有恶邻才行，与人交往也不必非要没有损友才行。只要能够把握好自己，恶邻和损友一样都是可以使你有所受益的。

【English Translation】

When choosing a place to reside, it is unnecessary to take as a decisive factor where there must be no wicked ones in neighborhood. Similarly, when engaged in social communications, it is unnecessary to ascertain that the persons whom you are to meet should be of no evil. If you only bear yourself with fortitude, you will not slip in benefiting from the both cases.

27. 君子小人 五更检点

27. To affirm if you are a noble man or a mean fellow, you'd better examine yourself in the early morning.

要知自家是君子小人，只须五更头①检点②，思想的是什么便得。

【中文注释】　① 五更头：五更是凌晨三时至五时。泛指一人清早。
　　　　　　　② 检点：此处指自我检讨。

【今文解译】　要想知道自己是君子还是小人，只消清晨醒来自我反省一下，检查一下脑子里在想些什么，便一清二楚。

【English Translation】

To affirm if you yourself are a noble man or a mean fellow, you only have to examine yourself early in the morning when you wake up. The answer just lies in what you are thinking about or desiring for.

28. 以道窒欲　则心自清

28. Put your desire under the control of ethical principles, and you will naturally have a pure heart.

以理听言，则中有主；以道窒欲，则心自清。

【今文解译】　以理性的态度听取大家的意见，凡事你就会自有主张。
　　　　　　　以伦理道德约束自己的欲望，你的心境自然就会清明。

【English Translation】

Listen carefully to the public opinions in a rational manner, and you will be the ruler of yourself in everything.

Put your desire under the control of ethical principles, and you will naturally have a pure heart.

29. 先达后近　交友道也

29. First be communicative and then be friendly with, — this is the way of making friends.

先淡后浓，先疏后亲，先达后近，交友道也。

【今文解译】　先淡薄而后浓厚，先疏远而后密切，先了解而后亲近。——
这些都是交友之道。

【English Translation】

First be indifferent to and then be considerate towards; first keep at a distance and then get close to; first be communicative and then be friendly with. — All these are the rules for making friends and the ways to get along with them.

30. 形骸非亲　大地亦幻

30. The body we have will no longer be ours in the end; the earth is nothing but a world of illusions.

形骸非亲，何况形骸外之长物；大地亦幻，何况大地内之微尘。

【今文解译】　连自己的身体都不尽属自己，而况身外的万事万物。
连大地本身都是虚幻的，而况大地上的微小颗粒物。

【English Translation】

The body we have will no longer be ours in the end, let alone the things outside our persons.

The earth is nothing but a world of illusions, much less the particles in it.

31. 寂而常惺　惺而常寂

31. Be clear-headed when in quiet and be quiet when clear-headed.

寂而常惺^①，寂寂之境不扰；惺而常寂，惺惺之念不弛^②。

【中文注释】　① 惺：清醒。
　　　　　　　② 不弛：使不被废弛。

【今文解译】　寂静时要常保持清醒,这样寂静的心境才不至于受干扰。
　　　　　　　清醒时要常保持平静,如此清醒的头脑才不至于被忽悠。

【English Translation】

Be clear-headed when in quiet so that the quietude can be free from disturbance.
Be quiet when clear-headed so that the clear-headedness can be well preserved.

32. 童子智少　少而愈完

32. Children know little about the world, so the less their knowledge the more intact their inborn nature.

童子智少，愈少而愈完；成人智多，愈多而愈散。

【今文解译】　孩子的心智不健全，而心智越不健全，其天性就越是纯然。
成人的心智发达，而心智越发达，其思想就越是活泛纷杂。

【English Translation】

Children know little about the world, so, the less their knowledge the more intact their inborn nature.
Adults know much about the world, so, the more their knowledge the more complicated their minds.

33. 常思考　多检点

33. Try hard to develop a habit of thinking diligently and self-reflecting frequently.

　　无事便思有闲杂念头否，有事便思有粗浮意气否；得意便思有骄矜辞色否，失意便思有怨望情怀否。时时检点得到，从多入少，从有入无，才是学问的真消息。

【今文解译】　闲来无事时要反思自己是否有乱七八糟的念头，有事忙碌时要反思自己是否有粗俗浮躁的意气，得意时要反思自己对人有没有颐指气使的腔调，失意时要反思自己是否有怨天尤人的情绪。——时时这样检讨自己，渐渐由多到少、从有入无地将反思所发现的问题统统解决掉，这样的修养功夫才称得上是名副其实的。

【English Translation】

Ask yourself the following: if you have any distracting thought when unoccupied, or if you are impetuous or ill-considered when occupied; if you boss others about when pleased with yourself, or if you become resentful when dissatisfied. — Self-examination repeatedly done like this can be called a real cultivation by which progress of perfection is made little by little and step by step.

34. 脱厌如释重　带恋如担枷

34. Out of poverty, the poor die content; burdened with wealth, the rich remain in fetters all their life.

　　贫贱之人，一无所有，及临命终时，脱一厌字；富贵之人，无所不有，及临命终时，带一恋字。脱一厌字，如释重负；带一恋字，如担枷锁。

【今文解译】　　穷人一无所有，临当寿终时，他们挣脱的是对贫穷的厌恶；富人无所不有，临当寿终时，他们却还对自己的财产恋恋不舍。挣脱贫穷使穷人如释重负；对财产的恋恋不舍使富人到死都还像枷锁缠身一样。

【English Translation】

Poor people have nothing to their names; but when lying on death bed, they congratulate themselves on being able to shake off poverty. Rich people have everything they desire; but when at the end of their lives, they still cannot lay down the burden of wealth. Thanks to being free from poverty, the poor die content. Burdened with wealth, the rich remain in fetters till their last breath.

35. 透得名利关　透得生死关

35. Free yourself from the desire for fame and gain and penetrate the issue of life and death.

透得名利关，只是小休歇；透得生死关，方是大休歇。

【今文解译】　看透名利只是小解脱，看透生死才是大解脱。

【English Translation】

It's only a short break if one can free oneself from the desire for fame and gain, but a long break indeed if one can penetrate the issue of life and death.

36. 多躁者　必无沉潜之识

36. A man of impetuous disposition has no deep insight.

多躁者，必无沉潜之识；多畏者，必无卓越之见；多欲者，必无慷慨之节；多言者，必无笃实之心；多勇者，必无文学之雅。

【今文解译】　　性情浮躁的人一定没有深刻敏锐的眼力。
畏首畏尾的人一定没有卓越超群的识见。
贪得无厌的人一定没有义薄云天的慷慨。
夸夸其谈的人一定没有诚恳笃实的心地。
勇武有余的人一定没有好文喜诗的雅致。

【English Translation】

The men of impetuous disposition are bound to have no deep insight.

The chicken-hearted men are bound to have no supreme vision.

The men with too many material desires are bound to have no generous character.

The men indulging in verbiage are bound to have no loyal and sincere mind.

The men full of sheer masculine strength are bound to have no culture in literature.

37. 佳思忽来　书能下酒

37. When a good frame of mind suddenly emerges, even a book can be a dish to go with wine.

佳思忽来，书能下酒；侠情一往，云可赠人。

【今文解译】　心情蓦然转好的时候，手中的书本也能拿来当下酒菜。
豪情万丈的时候，天上的云彩也可摘下来当礼物送人。

【English Translation】

When a good frame of mind suddenly emerges, even a book can be a dish to go with wine.

When the exuberant spirits run high, even a wisp of cloud can be taken as a souvenir to friend.

38. 生死老病　谁能透过

38. Without a deep understanding of the world, who can see through the implications of life and death, old and sick?

　　人不得道，生死老病四字关，谁能透过？独美人名将，老病之状，尤为可怜。

【今文解译】　生老病死是人生四大关卡，人若不彻悟其道，又怎能看得透？尤其是那些名满天下的美女和战将，他们的老境和病状尤其令人唏嘘。

【English Translation】

Without a deep understanding of the way of the world, how can one see through the implications of life and death, old and sick? As a matter of fact, the beauties with no peril and the generals with no enemy, when old and sick, are most pitiful.

39. 真放肆不在饮酒高歌

39. To be truly free and natural, one does not have to drink and chant with wide abandon.

　　真放肆不在饮酒高歌，假矜持偏于大庭卖弄。看明世事透，自然不重功名；认得当下真，是以常寻乐地。

【今文解译】　　真正的不拘形迹不在于举杯豪饮引吭高歌。
　　　　　　　　装出来的矜持偏爱在大庭广众下惺惺作态。
　　　　　　　　能将世事看透的，自然不会在乎什么功名。
　　　　　　　　能认清现实的，哪儿都是愉悦身心的乐土。

【 English Translation 】

To be truly free and natural, one does not have to drink and chant with wide abandon.
One who feigns himself serious tends to behave solemnly in manner on public occasions.
One who has seen through the vanity of the world naturally would not care about honor and rank.
One who has clearly recognized the situations confronted can find the land of bliss anywhere.

40. 人生待足何时足

40. When will it be the time if one only stops to feel fully satisfied?

人生待足何时足，未老得闲始是闲。

【今文解译】 觉得满足了才肯罢休，这要等到猴年马月啊？
人未老迈就能安享清闲，这才是真正的清闲。

【English Translation】

When will it be the time if one only stops to feel fully satisfied?
The leisure one obtains when not yet old enough is a real leisure.

41. 云烟影里见真身

41. Only amidst the shadows of clouds and mists can one see one's real self.

　　云烟影里见真身①，始悟形骸②为桎梏；禽鸟声中闻自性，方知情识是戈矛。

【中文注释】　① 真身：真正的自我。
　　　　　　② 形骸：佛教用语。肉身，即人的躯骸。

【今文解译】　云罩雾绕中看到了自己的真身，才明白躯骸其实只是束缚人的枷锁。
　　　　　　声声鸟叫中听到了自己的本性，才知道情欲识见原都是伤人的戈矛。

【 English Translation 】

Only when seeing one's real self amidst the shadows of clouds and mists can one realize that the body one has is just an object resembling fetters and manacles.
Only when understanding the rhythm of self-nature among the twitters of birds can one know that human passions and intelligence are but wounding spears.

42. 明霞可爱　瞬眼辄空

42. The bright sun rays will soon come to naught though they look lovely.

　　明霞①可爱，瞬眼而辄空②；流水堪听，过耳而不恋。人能以明霞视美色，则业障③自轻；人能以流水听弦歌，则性灵④何害。

【中文注释】　　① 明霞：晨昏时分明媚的阳光。
　　　　　　　　② 辄空：动不动就会消失。
　　　　　　　　③ 业障：佛教术语。意指妨碍修行的罪恶。
　　　　　　　　④ 性灵：指人的灵魂、精神、性情、情感等。

【今文解译】　　绚丽的明霞壮观可爱，但转眼间就会消失得无影无踪；流水的潺潺声悦耳动听，但流水却不会因为悦耳而停滞不前。人若能像眼睛观赏明霞那样看待美色，那么贪恋美色的罪过也就不会那么深重；人若能像耳朵聆听流水声那样聆听音乐，那么音乐中的靡靡之声也就不会影响到自己的性灵。

【English Translation】

The bright sun rays will soon come to naught though they look lovely. The murmuring of running water will never remain though it is pleasant to the ear. It would not be a sin so seriously regarded if you can admire the beauty of a woman in the way you watch the bright sun rays. It would cause the soul no harm if you can appreciate music and songs in the way you listen to the murmuring of running water.

43. 不怀好意者　我自不理会

43. Ignore the one who doesn't mean well.

　　寒山^①诗云:"有人来骂我,分明了了知,虽然不应对,却是得便宜^②。"
此言宜深玩味。

【中文注释】　　① 寒山: 即寒山子, 唐代贞观年间的高僧, 好吟词偈, 参
　　　　　　　　禅顿悟, 体会甚深。
　　　　　　　② 得便宜: 隐喻 "从中获益" 或 "引以为鉴"。

【今文解译】　　寒山子有诗云:"有人来找我骂架,他的来意我心知肚明。
　　　　　　　虽然我没有还口,但得便宜的却是我。"这几句话的深意
　　　　　　　值得玩味。

【English Translation】

Master Hanshan* wrote in one of his poems, which goes, "Somebody has
come to insult me. To me his intention is crystal clear. With no response from
my side, I'm nevertheless favored by his gear." How meaningful the lines!

【English Annotation】

* Master Hanshan (?-?): A famous hermit during the reign of Zhenguan (627-
649) of the Tang Dynasty, well known in poetry.

44. 有誉于前　不若无毁于后

44. Seeking praise in the presence of people is not as good as avoiding vilification from behind your back.

有誉于前，不若无毁于后；有乐于身，不若无忧于心。

【今文解译】　希望别人当面夸赞你，不如避免有人背后诋毁你。
耽于肉体上的快乐，不如追求心灵上的无忧无虑。

【English Translation】

Seeking praise in the presence of people is not as good as avoiding vilification from behind your back.

Leaving your mind free of fears and worries is better than indulging in physical pleasures.

45. 无稽之言　是在不听听耳

45. Talks with no ground to stand on are not worthwhile to take seriously even if you overheard about them.

会心之语，当以不解解之；无稽之言，是在不听听耳。

【今文解译】　应该用心去领会的话，本就不该用言语去解读。
　　　　　　　对待无根无据的言论，最好的办法是不予理会。

【English Translation】

Remarks knowing to the heart need no explanation in language even if you can find a proper wording to do so.
Talks with no ground to stand on are not worthwhile to take seriously even if you have overheard about them.

46. 拨开才是手段　立定方见脚跟

46. Eliminate the interference of vanity and hold your foot firmly in the raging wind and rain.

花繁柳密^①处拨得开，才是手段^②；风狂雨急^③时立得定，方见脚跟。

【中文注释】　① 花繁柳密: 隐指声色迷乱、充满诱惑的环境。
② 手段: 泛指技巧、能力、方法等。
③ 风狂雨急: 隐指条件艰苦、环境恶劣等。

【今文解译】　花柳丛中能拨开繁密的枝叶, 自如地行走其间, 这才是真本事。
风狂雨急的时候能不畏艰险, 始终站稳脚跟, 这才看得出立场。

【English Translation】

A good performance can only be affirmed when one moves freely through the density of flowers and willows.
A steadfast foothold can only be recognized when one stands firmly in the raging wind and rain.

47. 身在事外　宜悉利害

47. To comment on a matter none of your business, you should first find out all the right and wrong causes in it.

议事者身在事外，宜悉利害之情；任事者身居事中，当忘利害之虑。

【今文解译】　谈论事情的人，由于是置身事外，所以开口前最好先弄清楚是非曲直。

在做事情的人，由于是身在其中，所以最好不要患得患失、斤斤计较。

【English Translation】

To comment on a matter one has nothing to do with, one should first endeavor to find out all the right and wrong causes in it.

To deal with a matter one is personally engaged in, one should cast off all the considerations of the gains and losses of his own.

48. 谈空反被空迷

48. Those who are fond of talking about phantoms are finally confused by the phantoms.

谈空^①反被空迷^②，耽静多为静缚。

【中文注释】　① 谈空：空，空寂之道。谈空也即谈论空寂之道。
　　　　　　　② 空迷：被空寂之道所迷惑。

【今文解译】　谈论空寂之道的反而会被万法皆空所迷惑。
　　　　　　　整日沉浸于静境中的大多会被静境所束缚。

【English Translation】

Those who are fond of talking about phantoms are finally confused by the phantoms.

Those who are persistently indulgent in tranquility are often bound up by the tranquility.

49. 贫不足羞　贱不足恶

49. It's not a shame to be poor and not a disgrace to be humble.

　　贫不足羞，可羞是贫而无志；贱不足恶，可恶是贱而无能；老不足叹，可叹是老而虚生；死不足悲，可悲是死而无补。

【今文解译】　　贫穷并不丢脸，丢脸的是家徒四壁且还没有志气。
卑贱并不令人厌恶，令人厌恶的是卑贱且还无能。
年老并不可叹，可叹的是人及耄耋却还无所作为。
死亡并不可悲，可悲的是至死都还没有一得之功。

【English Translation】

It is not a shame to be poor, but a shame indeed if one has no aspiration because of being poor.

It is not a disgrace to be humble, but a disgrace indeed if one ever remains incapable on account of his humbleness.

It is not lamentable to get old, but lamentable indeed if one has achieved nothing when old enough.

It is not pathetic to have a death, but pathetic indeed if one has never done anything good to the world till death.

50. 彼无望德　此无示恩

50. You expect me no favor and I show you no kindness.

　　彼无望德，此无示恩，穷交所以能长；望不胜奢，欲不胜餍，利交所以必伤。

【今文解译】　　你无求于我，我亦不施恩于你。这种淡如水的交情之所以能够长久，原因就在于此。

　　　　　　　　总想从别人那儿得到更多好处。这种得陇望蜀的交情之所以脆弱，原因就在于此。

【English Translation】

You expect me no favor and I show you no kindness. — Relationship so indifferently established can ever last.

Ceaselessly expect extra favors and charities from fellow beings. — Relationship so solely for benefit is vulnerable.

51. 当为情死　不当为情怨

51. One can die for love but should not resent it.

　　语云：当为情死，不当为情怨。关乎情者，原可死而不可怨者也。虽然既云情矣，此身已为情有，又何忍死耶？然不死终不透彻耳。君平之柳①，崔护之花②，汉宫之流叶③，蜀女之飘梧④，令后世有情之人咨嗟想慕，托之语言，寄之歌咏。而奴无昆仑⑤，客无黄衫⑥，知己无押衙⑦，同志无虞侯⑧，则虽盟在海棠，终是陌路萧郎⑨耳。

【中文注释】
① 君平之柳：君平是唐代诗人韩翃的字。"君平之柳"是指他的爱妾柳氏。柳氏在战乱中被敌军掳去，同府的虞侯许俊为他抢回。

② 崔护之花：崔护是唐代诗人。"崔护之花"说的是崔护有一年清明节到城外郊游，路上因口渴而到一户人家要水喝，那家女子的热情好客使崔护印象深刻，以致来年清明诗人故地重游时再次来到那家人的门前，不料发现门户紧锁，于是就在门上题诗一首："去年今日此门中，人面桃花相映红。人面不知何处去，桃花依旧笑春风。"

③ 汉宫之流叶：唐代宫女韩翠屏在红叶上题诗，红叶被流水冲到宫外，学士于祐捡到后，又在红叶上题诗流回宫内，韩翠屏复捡得此叶。后来宫中放出三千宫女，于祐得以娶韩翠屏为妾。韩翠屏的红叶题诗曰："流水何太急，深宫尽日闲。殷勤谢红叶，好去到人间。"于祐的回题诗曰："曾闻叶上题红怨，叶上题诗寄阿谁？"

④ 蜀女之飘梧：是指《梧桐叶》中记述的西蜀人任继图与妻子李云英分离后李云英题诗在梧桐叶上被任继图捡得而夫妻团圆的故事。

⑤ 奴无昆仑：唐代传奇短篇小说《昆仑奴》中一个昆仑奴为其主人劫得心仪女子的故事。

⑥ 客无黄衫：唐代传奇短篇小说《霍小玉传》中一位身着黄衫的游侠如何将负心郎带至霍小玉面前听其历数自己的不幸和对方的负心的故事。

⑦ 知己无押衙: 唐代传奇短篇小说《无双记》中一个押衙如何帮助王仙客和无双终成眷属的故事。

⑧ 同志无虞侯: 虞侯许俊如何为同府的韩翊夺回被掳走爱妾的故事。

⑨ 萧郎: 泛指古代女子所钟爱的男子。

【今文解译】 有句话是这么说的: 可以为情而死, 而不应当为情而怨。男女之间的情事, 本就是可死不可怨的。不过话又说回来了, 既然已经与人共浴爱河, 又怎么忍心去死?! 然而不以死明志, 又怎么能体现爱之深切?! 君平之柳、崔护之花、汉宫之流叶以及蜀女之飘梧, 这些故事后世有情之人看了一个个都赞叹艳羡不已, 纷纷将它们形诸文字, 广为传颂。但是从另一方面说, 要是没有昆仑奴那样的忠诚老仆、黄衫客那样的热肠游侠、监狱看守那样的肝胆义士以及虞侯那样的生死兄弟, 为情男怨女们挺身而出, 成全他们的心愿, 纵使再有什么海棠花下的山盟海誓, 他们终究还是无缘走到一起去的。

【 English Translation 】

There is a saying which runs: One can die for love but should not resent it. So far as the relationship between sexes is concerned, it is quite reasonable for the ones who have fallen in love to sacrifice for each other rather than to resent each other. Nevertheless, having a sweetheart at pillow-side, how can one have the heart to die in vain? And except death is there any other means worthy to be used to express true love? The tales such as a wife captured in wartime finally saved, a female benefactor ever missed by her male beneficiary, the love messages written on a fallen leaf secretly floating to and fro in the water of the Han* palace drain, and the reunion of a separated couple in the land of Shu*, are all romantic stuffs which made many of the affectionate men and women of the later eras sigh with admiration, form them in words, and spread them widely with chant. But on the other hand, if there had been no loyal slave of Kunlun* who rescued the pretty girl fancied by his master, no knight-errant clad in yellow who sought out the fellow betraying his fiancé, no gallant jailor who helped an infatuated male in his marriage with a lady of his heart, or no companion who seized back the beloved concubine for his friend, even if with sweet oaths of long-lasting love sworn in the presence of the cherry-apple trees, the men and women in love would not be able to have the luck to celebrate their reunion in the end.

【 English Annotation 】

* The Han: Referred to the Han Dynasty lasting from 206BC to AD220.
* The land of Shu: Generally referred to the land of today's Sichuan Province.
* Kunlun: A place referred to the area including Indonesia and Malaysia since ancient times.

52. 缩不尽相思地 补不完离恨天

52. For the lovers at parting or in two places, there is bitterness unspeakable.

费长房^①缩不尽相思地，女娲氏^②补不完离恨天。

【中文注释】 ① 费长房：古代传说中能用他手上的缩地鞭把远在天边
的地方缩到自己眼前或者把两个相隔万里的地方缩到一
起的神仙。
② 女娲氏：古代神话中用彩石补天的女神。

【今文解译】 费长房虽有缩地的法术，但却无法拉近两地相思者之间
的距离。
女娲氏虽有补天的神功，但却无法修复爱人分离后留下
的缺憾。

【English Translation】

Master Fei* is able to shorten the distance between two different places, but not in a position to bring together the lovers far apart.
Nüwa* can mend the broken sky with colorful stones, but not capable of mending the cracked hearts of the ones bitterly separated.

【English Annotation】

* Master Fei: An ancient legendary figure named Fei Zhangfang who is said to have the ability to move a place far away to his own presence or shorten the distance between two different places far apart with a powerful whip.
* Nüwa: A legendary goddess in ancient Chinese mythology, best known for creating mankind and repairing the wall of heaven.

53. 梦醒心不归

53. The dream is finished but the heart yearning for the love is still lingering in the dreamland.

枕边梦去心亦去，醒后梦还心不还。

【今文解译】　心随着梦去见意中人，醒后梦回来了，可心却没有。

【English Translation】

For a meeting with the dear gone is the heart with dream, but after wake-up the dream returns while the heart is still lingering in the dreamland.

54. 我幸在不痴不慧中

54. I congratulate myself on being in the middle between the wise and the stupid.

阮籍^①邻家少妇，有美色，当垆沽酒^②，籍常诣饮^③，醉便卧其侧。隔帘闻坠钗声，而不动念者，此人不痴则慧，我幸在不痴不慧中。

【中文注释】　① 阮籍: 三国魏文学家、思想家,"竹林七贤"之一, 才华横溢, 性情豪放怪诞。
② 当垆沽酒: 垆, 酒店里安放酒瓮的土台子, 借指酒店。当垆沽酒就是开酒铺卖酒。
③ 诣饮: 诣, 到某个地方去。诣饮, 此处指到邻家少妇的酒店里去喝酒。

【今文解译】　阮籍家隔壁有个少妇,十分貌美, 沿街开有一家酒铺。阮籍是那儿的常客, 每回喝醉了便躺在她身旁不走了。隔着帘子听见钗子落地的声音而不起邪念, 这样的人不是呆子就是慧者。我庆幸自己既不是呆子也不是慧者。

【English Translation】

A good-looking married young woman had a wine shop next door. Ruan Ji* often went there for a drink and fell asleep right beside her when dead drunk. One who hears through the curtain the sound produced by a hairpin falling to the ground and yet gives no loose rein to his fancy must be a wise man if not a stupid one. I just congratulate myself on being in the middle between the wise and the stupid.

【English Annotation】

* Ruan Ji (210-263): Styled Sizong, a poet, writer and thinker of the Wei Kingdom during the Three Kingdoms Period and one of the leaders of the Seven Worthies of the Bamboo Grove, who pursued the philosophy combining the doctrines of Taoism and Confucianism.

55. 出相思海　下离恨天

55. A merciful raft or an affectional ladder may save the separated lovers from deep lovesickness.

慈悲筏，济人出相思海；恩爱梯，接人下离恨天。

【今文解译】　用慈悲做成的筏子可以渡人驶出相思无边的海洋。

用恩爱做成的梯子可以接人走下离恨绵绵的苍穹。

【English Translation】

The raft equipped with mercy can be used to ferry the men and women longing for each other out of the sea of lovesickness.

The ladder made of conjugal affection can be used to help bringing together the lovers sorrowfully separated in two places.

56. 花柳藏淑女　雨云襄王梦

56. A nice lady amid flowers and willows can never be traced while rain and clouds had never attended the King.

花柳深藏淑女居，何殊三千弱水①；雨云②不入襄王梦③，空忆十二巫山④。

【中文注释】　① 三千弱水：古时候许多浅而湍急的河流不能用舟船而只能用皮筏过渡，古人认为是由于水羸弱而不能载舟，因此把这样的河流叫作弱水。继而，文人逐渐用"弱水"来泛指险而遥远的河流。

② 云雨：也即巫山云雨，隐喻男欢女爱。

③ 襄王梦：襄王，即楚襄王。据宋玉《神女赋》，楚襄王夜梦神女并追求神女却被洁身自持的神女拒绝。神女"欢情未接，将辞而去"，楚襄王被拒绝后则伤感失意之下泪流不止，苦苦等待直到天明。因而，"襄王梦"这个典故具有求爱不成、求欢不得，或失恋、单相思的意味。

④ 十二巫山：即巫山十二峰，意指美女或仙女。

【今文解译】　淑女幽居在花柳深闺，像三千弱水一样难以到达。

神女不肯入梦来，襄王空想巫山十二峰又有何用。

【English Translation】

The boudoir of a charming lady deep amid the flowers and willows can never be traced, just like the shallow waters three thousand miles beyond the distant Isle Penglai*, no one has set foot there.

The goddess in charge of the employment of rain and clouds* never appeared in King Xiang's dream*. What's the use for His Majesty to dream in vain the Twelve Peaks along the Long River*?

【English Annotation】

* Isle Penglai: Sometimes related to an isle and sometimes to a mountain on it,

a fabled abode of immortals on the Bohai Sea in Chinese legendary literature.

* Rain and clouds: Often used as a metaphor to indicate love affairs between man and woman.

* King Xiang's dream: The king is referring to King Xiang of Chu (329BC-263BC) who courted a fair woman he came across in his dream and was rejected; King Xiang's dream is therefore meant for a dream of love, or simply as love in vain or one-sided love.

* The Twelve Peaks along the Long River: Referring to the peaks located on the banks of Yangtze River about 10 to 30 km away from the Wushan County. Six of them are on the northern bank, and the other six on the southern bank. Due to frequent rains and lack of sunshine, the Twelve Peaks are often surrounded by mist and clouds. Cruising along the peaks, you seem to enter a fairyland. In ancient literature, the Twelve Peaks are the symbols of fairy maidens.

57. 天若有情天亦老

57. If the heaven had a heart as humans, how old he would be today!

　　黄叶无风自落，秋云不雨长阴。天若有情天亦老，摇摇幽恨难禁。惆怅旧欢如梦，觉来无处追寻。

【中文注释】　此篇六句取自宋代词人孙洙的《河满子·秋怨》一词的下半阕，全词为："怅望浮生急景，凄凉宝瑟余音。楚客多情偏怨别，碧山远水登临。目送连天衰草，夜阑几处疏砧。// 黄叶无风自落，秋云不雨长阴。天若有情天亦老，摇摇幽恨难禁。惆怅旧欢如梦，觉来无处追寻。"

【今文解译】　枯叶即使无风也会自行飘落，秋云化不成雨就会带来长时间阴天。

天若是有情，天也会因情而衰老，最难忍是心中挥之不去的幽恨。

梦一般缠绵的旧欢，醒来时竟无处寻找。

【 English Translation 】

The withered leaves will fall themselves even without the blowing of wind. The autumn clouds, if not able to transform into rain, will gloom the sky for long.

If the heaven had a heart as humans, how old he would be today! It is always difficult to put up with the hidden resentment dangling in the heart.

How sorrowful it is that the old happiness is just like a dream! People have nowhere to look for it when they wake up.

58. 绝代美女　终归黄土

58. Even the peerless goddesses like Xishi will become piles of soil in the end.

吴妖小玉①飞作烟，越艳西施②化为土。

【中文注释】　① 吴妖小玉: 据说是吴王夫差的小女儿, 名紫玉, 生得妖媚动人, 因父亲阻拦未嫁成韩重而气绝身亡, 入殓后化作烟雾消失不见了。
② 越艳西施: 春秋晚期越国的浣纱女西施, 具有"沉鱼"之美。

【今文解译】　吴宫的紫玉和越国的西施都是绝代美女, 而今一个化作了烟雾, 一个变成了黄土。

【English Translation】

Just as the most attractive Ziyu of Wu* turned into a wisp of smoke, so the most beautiful Xishi of Yue* a double handful of soil.

【English Annotation】

* Ziyu of Wu: Youngest daughter of King Fuchai of Wu, who loved and intended to marry Han Chong, a Taoist scholar, but failed because of the king's disagreement. Ziyu grieved so much over her father's opposition that she died of deep resentment and transformed into smoke at last.
* Xishi of Yue: A silk-washing maid of the state of Yue towards the end of the Spring and Autumn Period. Her beauty believed to be capable of sinking fish or making fish forgetting to swim.

59. 杨柳沾啼痕 三叠唱离恨

59. Grief at parting and sorrow of separation are always the eternal theme of poetry.

几条杨柳，沾来多少啼痕①；三叠阳关，唱彻古今离恨②。

【中文注释】 ① 第一句：自西汉以来，柳枝就一直被文人墨客用作送别亲友的纪念物以及寄托送别之情的信物的代名词。
② 第二句：三叠阳关，也即《阳关三叠》，琴曲名，亦称《阳关曲》或《渭城曲》，是根据唐代诗人王维的七言绝句《送元二使安西》谱写的一首著名的艺术歌曲，描写离别之情。因全曲分三段，原诗反复三次，故称"三叠"。后泛指送别之曲。

【今文解译】 几根送别用的柳条，上面沾着的尽是亲朋好友分手时留下的泪痕。
一曲《阳关三叠》凄婉的歌词，唱尽了古往今来生离死别的哀怨。

【English Translation】

The twigs plucked from the willow trees* are unexceptionally stained with the tear marks of the ones at parting.
Since ancient times, the farewell song of *Yang Guan San Die** has been sung to pour out the nostalgic feelings.

【English Annotation】

* Willow twigs: A substance which had been frequently used as a farewell present to the parting ones in the dynasties of Han and Tang. As the traditional understanding has it, the suppleness and long length of the fresh twigs were in a power to give expression to the sentiments of those who were on send-off for those who were leaving.
* *Yang Guan San Die*: An art song originated from the Tang poet Wang Wei's poem titled *Seeing Yuan the Second off to the Northwest Frontier*, which airs the poet's deep grief over his seeing off Yuan the second.

60. 弄柳拈花　尽是销魂之处

60. Play with beautiful women, and what you gain will be no more than the soul-consuming pleasures.

　　弄绿绮之琴①，焉得文君②之听；濡彩毫之笔，难描京兆之眉③。瞻云望月，无非凄怆之声；弄柳拈花，尽是销魂之处。

【中文注释】　　① 绿绮之琴：绿绮是司马相如的琴名。司马相如，西汉辞赋家，以一曲《凤求凰》赢得卓文君的倾慕。
　　② 文君：富商卓吉善的女儿，因倾慕司马相如的才情而与其私奔。
　　③ 京兆之眉：汉代张敞任京兆尹（相当于今日首都的最高行政长官），夫妻间十分恩爱，常在家中为妻子画眉。

【今文解译】　　即便弹奏司马相如留下的琴，也未必能引得卓文君来垂听。
　　即便让眉笔蘸满颜料，也画不出张敞为其爱妻画眉的情意。
　　瞻云望月，听到的无非是凄凉悲怆的声音。
　　攀花摘柳，得到的不过是销魂的肌肤之亲。

【English Translation】

How can one draw Wenjun*'s attention even he plays the stringed instrument verily owned by Xiangru*?

One can never pencil the eyebrows of his love as Zhang Chang* did even if his brush is fully dipped with colored paste.

Gazing at the moon and clouds in the sky, what comes to your ears would be nothing but the sounds painful to your heart.

Playing with beautiful women, what you gain would be no more than the soul-consuming pleasures.

【 English Annotation 】

* Wenjun & * Xiangru: Wenjun, surnamed Zhuo; Xiangru, surnamed Sima. Sima Xiangru (c. 179BC-118BC) is an eminent poet of the Western Han Dynasty, and Zhuo Wenjun, a lady from a rich family who had been deserted by her former husband. One day, Xiangru paid a visit to Wenjun's father and played the zither at the request of the host. The plaintive tune of asking her hand upset the calmness in her heart. She went to Xiangru's room at night and made a solemn pledge of love to him, and then eloped with him without any hesitation. The romance of the two and their elopement have been considered the most renowned one in the Chinese history.

* Zhang Chang (?-48BC): A metropolitan governor of the Western Han Dynasty, well known for his penciling the eyebrows of his wife. From then on, the deed to pencil the eyebrows of one's wife or girlfriend has been considered as a deep love expressed by the husband or boyfriend.

61. 豆蔻不消心上恨

61. The cardamom spray would not easily release her love grievance from the heart.

豆蔻①不消心上恨，丁香空结雨中愁②。

【中文注释】　① 豆蔻：一种植物，代指少女。此典故首见于唐代诗人杜牧的诗："娉娉袅袅十三余，豆蔻梢头二月初。春风十里扬州路，卷上珠帘总不如。"
② 丁香花除了素雅清纯的美丽和沁人心脾的幽香之外，还因为它是爱情与幸福的象征，故常被人们誉为"爱情之花"或"幸福之花"。本句出自南唐中主李璟的词《摊破浣溪沙·手卷真珠上玉钩》："手卷真珠上玉钩，依前春恨锁重楼。风里落花谁是主？思悠悠。// 青鸟不传云外信，丁香空结雨中愁。回首绿波三楚暮，接天流。"由于"丁香体柔软"（详见杜甫的《江头五咏·丁香》），因此也常被后代的文人骚客用以隐喻女人的舌头。

【今文解译】　豆蔻少女心头的情怨迟迟不肯释怀，只为丁香花还在雨中孤零零地愁眉不展。

【English Translation】

The cardamom spray* would not release her love grievance from the heart, just because the clover* is still idling sorrowfully in the rain.

【English Annotation】

* The cardamom spray in China is referred to the young girls at the age of 13 or 14, who have just begun to understand love.
* The clover is referred to a flower representing love and happiness and has been often used as a code word for the tongue of a woman by literati in their works.

62. 截住巫山不放云

62. Block the valleys of Mount Wu, so as not to let the clouds float away.

填平湘岸都栽竹，截住巫山不放云。

【中文注释】 本篇通过"湘竹"和"巫山"两个典故抒发了恋爱中人们心中的爱情豪言。

【今文解译】 把湘江两岸都填平了栽满斑竹。
把巫山都封住了不让云飘出去。

【English Translation】

Fill and level up the bed of River Xiang*, thereby planting the mottled bamboos.
Block the valleys of Mount Wu*, thereby not letting the clouds float away.

【English Annotation】

* River Xiang: Also known as Xiang River, Xiangjiang or Xiangjiang River, a tributary of the Yangtze River, the longest river in Hunan Province. One of the ancient legends has it that the two concubines of King Shun, E'Huang and Nüying, who, upon hearing the emperor's death, sank themselves in the river, with their teardrops splashing on the bamboos nearby. It was in this way the two princesses expressed their loyal and constant love to the king, the story of which has been widely popularized in China.
* Mount Wu: A mountain sitting along the two banks of the Yangtze River, often literally used as a metaphor to symbolize the love between man and woman.

63. 那忍重看娃鬒绿

63. A deserted fair maid is not in the mood to gaze at her own face and hair in the mirror.

那忍重看娃鬒绿①，终期一遇客衫黄②。

【中文注释】　① 娃鬒绿：指年轻貌美女子的秀发。娃，吴地对漂亮姑娘的称谓。
② 客衫黄：即黄衫客。根据唐代传奇短篇小说《霍小玉传》，霍小玉痴情于李十郎，可李十郎是个负心汉。黄衫客见状抱不平，强扭李十郎至霍小玉寓所，使小玉见上了负心人一面，小玉对李十郎说："我为女子，薄命如斯！君是丈夫，负心若此！韶颜稚齿，饮恨而终。我死之后，必为厉鬼，使君妻妾，终日不安！"

【今文解译】　漂亮的姑娘再也无心对镜自赏，只盼着早点遇到一位打抱不平的侠客，帮她在负心汉面前出口恶气。

【 English Translation 】

A fair maid is not in the mood to gaze at her own face and hair in the mirror, only to expect a knight to come and help her out in her love with a fickle fellow.

64. 空闺哀怨　薄幸惊魂

64. The sadness of a deserted woman often makes the fickle man ashamed for his heartlessness.

　　幽情化而石立①，怨风结而冢青②；千古空闺之感，顿令薄幸惊魂。

【中文注释】　① 幽情化而石立：说的是望夫石的故事。
　　　　　　② 怨风结而冢青：说的是王昭君的故事。

【今文解译】　一往情深的妻子最后化作了山岗上的望夫石。
　　　　　　满腹哀怨的昭君最终变成了塞北的一堆青冢。
　　　　　　空守闺房的苦涩自古就令人哀叹，负心男子听了一定羞愧难当。

【English Translation】

Waiting for her husband far apart, a wife with longing eyes finally transformed into a stone standing on the hill.

Bearing her hatred towards the painter in vain, the court maiden turned out to be a pile of grave beyond the cold frontier.

The resentment such as above-mentioned in the long history, if let known to those fickle men, would surely make them ashamed for their heartlessness.

65. 良缘易合　知己难投

65. A good match is easy to make while a confidant, if no longer compatible, is hard to get along.

良缘易合，红叶亦可为媒；知己难投，白璧未能获主。

【今文解译】　能促成喜结良缘是件好事，哪怕是一片红叶也能为媒。
如果知己不再相投，就是白璧也无法找到赏识它的人。

【English Translation】

If a good match is applicable to bringing a man and a woman into holy matrimony, even a red leaf can be the go-between.

If confidants are no longer compatible, even a piece of white jade would fail to find its appreciator.

66. 蝶憩香风　尚多芳梦

66. Bathed in the fragrant wind, even an emotional butterfly will have sweet images in succession.

蝶憩香风，尚多芳梦；鸟沾红雨，不任娇啼。

【今文解译】　蝴蝶行停于芬芳的鲜花丛中，连睡觉时做的梦也都一个个带着香味。
当鸟的羽毛上落满凋零的花瓣，就再也听不到它们悦耳的娇啼声了。

【English Translation】

Bathed in the fragrant wind, even an emotional butterfly will have sweet images in succession.
Petals fallen onto the plume of a delicate bird make the twitter sound more unbearable.

67. 无端饮却相思水

67. A drink of acacia water and one will no longer believe that lovesickness can drive the lovers to death.

无端饮却相思水，不信相思想煞人。

【今文解译】 平白无故地饮下相思水，就不再相信相思真的能把人相思至死。

【English Translation】

Drink down acacia water for no reason, and you will no longer believe that lovesickness is able to drive the lovers to death.

68. 多情成恋　薄命何嗟

68. Amorous people tend to fall in love with the opposite sex, but some women would sigh with sorrow when ill-fated.

陌上繁华，两岸春风轻柳絮；闺中寂寞，一窗夜雨瘦梨花。芳草归迟①，青驹别易②，多情成恋③，薄命何嗟④。要亦人各有心，非关女德善怨⑤。

【中文注释】　① 芳草归迟：尽管已是芳草萋萋，可那人总不能早早归来。隐喻女子埋怨在外四处游历的心上人为何不早点回家。
② 青驹别易：骑在马背上道别很容易做到。
③ 多情成恋：多愁善感的人容易心生恋情。
④ 薄命何嗟：红颜多薄命，嗟叹又有何用。
⑤ 女德善怨：女人天生就好抱怨叫屈，怨天尤人。

【今文解译】　小路两旁花开似锦，河流两岸春风吹拂，柳絮轻扬。待字闺中的姑娘寂寞难耐，一夜风雨后竟变得比梨花还瘦。盼君早归但总也不归，马背上别后却一走千里，多情的总是求欢得爱，命薄的又何苦哀叹不已。其实这些都和恋爱中的女人好怨天尤人无关，如果非要说有什么关系，那也是：每个人对爱情都各有各的感受。

【English Translation】

In full bloom are the roadside flowers, and from the two river banks there fly out the tiny willow catkins on spring wind.
The girl in the literary boudoir is lonely and becomes thinner than the pear blossoms after a night of rain.
A traveler's homecoming is postponed again and again though his dearest is earnestly awaiting him, while on horseback it's easy to bid farewell mutually.
Amorous people tend to fall in love with the opposite sex, but some emotional women would sigh with sadness when ill-fated. Actually, it has nothing to do with the women that are liable to adopt a sentimental pose when in love, but really something to do with the fact that everyone has his own feelings when experiencing love.

69. 清风好伴　明月故人

69. A gust of fresh breeze can be a good companion and an old friend, the emitting moon.

幽堂昼深，清风忽来好伴；虚窗夜朗，明月不减故人。

【今文解译】　深深的厅堂在白昼里显得特别幽静,忽然拂来一阵清风,
似有好友来到我的身旁。
推开关着的窗户, 举头仰望晴朗的夜空, 只见明月当头,
一如故人情义不减当年。

【 English Translation 】

The deep living room, so quiet and solitary even in daylight, is suddenly passed by a gust of fresh breeze, as if a good companion has come to pay me a visit.

Through the opened window, I look up at the emitting moon hanging on the clear sky, as if seeing an old friend who is as cordial as ever.

70. 平生云水心　春花秋月语

70. To a person who adores the beauty of nature, autumn moon and spring flowers are always the only subject.

　　初弹如珠后如缕，一声两声落花雨；诉尽平生云水心^①，尽是春花秋月^②语。

【中文注释】　① 云水心："云"与"水"除了本义之外，此处可以理解为"漫游如行云流水一般"，也可以简单理解成"大自然"的意思。云水心，也即将自己的情思寄托于漂流不定的云水之间。
② 春花秋月：此处喻男女之间的情事。

【今文解译】　落花时节下的雨，初下时像珠玉落盘叮叮咚咚，而后便细如丝线缕缕不绝；如果让这雨把云水般绵绵的柔情蜜意都倾诉尽，话题无非就是春花秋月。

【English Translation】

The rain first falls like pearls and then like threads; together with the rain drops also fall a few blossoms from twigs. If the rain is let thoroughly air its lifelong feelings about the clouds and water, the autumn moon and spring flowers* would be the only topic.

【English Annotation】

* The autumn moon and spring flowers: Here referred to the romance between man and woman or love affairs between sexes.

71. 封疆缩地　中庭歌舞犹喧

71. The sissy men at court sing and dance to their hearts' content while the frontiers are in decline.

料今天下皆妇人矣。封疆缩其地，而中庭之歌舞犹喧；战血枯其人，而满座貂蝉自若。我辈书生，既无诛乱讨贼之柄，而一片报国之忱，惟于寸楮尺字间见之。使天下之须眉面妇人者，亦耸然有起色。

【今文解译】　当今天下的男人一个个都和妇人一般。国土在一寸寸沦丧，可他们的殿堂里却依旧是歌舞升平；战场上将士们在浴血奋战，可他们身边如云的美女却毫无惊慌之色。我们都是书生，没有戡乱平叛的权柄，但我们可以拿起笔把我们报效国家的赤诚之心写在纸上，以期唤醒朝中那些娘娘腔的男人们，也能拿出点做男人的样子来。

【English Translation】

In my opinion, today's men at court are all sissyish. They sing and dance to their hearts' content in the magnificent halls while the frontiers are being lost one after another. They have fair maids to attend their grand parties as if nothing had happened while the generals and soldiers are fighting to the last drop of their blood along the borders. We scholars, with warm hearts to serve our country, but not entitled to make war on the invaders, can only write with pens to express our deep concern for the situation, hoping that all the sissy men at court will be aroused from indifference and show up as real men.

72. 士不晓廉耻　衣冠狗彘

72. Scholar-knights who have no sense of shame and dignity are only dogs and pigs in hat and clothes.

人不通古今，襟裾马牛；士不晓廉耻，衣冠狗彘。

【今文解译】　为人不通古今，那就是褂袍加身的牛马。

　　　　　　　为士不知廉耻，那就是穿衣戴帽的猪狗。

【English Translation】

Folks who have no knowledge about the past and present are but horses and cows in man's garb.

Scholar-knights who have no sense of shame and dignity are only dogs and pigs in hat and clothes.

73. 宁以风霜自挟　毋为鱼鸟亲人

73. The man of integrity would rather go through all the hardships on their own than act as the pooled fish or caged bird totally dependent on human beings for living.

苍蝇附骥，捷则捷矣，难辞处后之羞①；茑萝②依松，高则高矣，未免仰攀之耻。所以君子宁以风霜自挟，毋为鱼鸟亲人。

【中文注释】　① 处后之羞: 此处意为趴在靠近屁股的马尾上那种羞耻。
② 茑萝: 一种能爬蔓的落叶小乔木, 尤喜攀爬松树。

【今文解译】　苍蝇趴在马的尾巴上疾驰, 速度快是快了, 但不免有处后之羞。茑萝缠绕着松树蔓生, 长得高是高了, 但不免有仰攀之耻。因此, 君子宁愿靠自己的力量去抗击风霜严寒, 也不愿像池鱼笼鸟那样依赖人类。

【English Translation】

Flies attached to the tail of a horse can move as fast as the horse but can hardly absolve themselves of the disgrace to be so close to the horse-hip. Vines twining around the trunk of a cypress can be as tall as the cypress but can hardly be dispensed of the shame to seek high position by relying on outside force. Therefore, the man of moral integrity would rather go through all the storms and frosts on their own than act as the pooled fish or caged bird totally depending on human beings for living.

74. 仕夫贪财好货　乃有爵之乞丐

74. A high-ranking official, if merely interested in seeking material gains, is a beggar with title of nobility.

平民种德施惠，是无位之公卿；士夫贪财好货，乃有爵之乞丐。

【今文解译】　　普通百姓若能积德行善，堪称没有爵位的公卿大臣。
　　　　　　　　身居高位但唯利是图，只能是挂着爵位头衔的乞丐。

【English Translation】

An ordinary person, if able to bestow benevolence on others, can be addressed as a duke without rank.

A high-ranking official, if merely interested in seeking material gains, is a beggar with title of nobility.

75. 一失足成千古恨

75. A false slip may cause a lifelong regret.

一失足为千古恨，再回头是百年人。

【今文解译】 有些错误犯不得，一犯就会成为终身的遗憾；即使再回头，人事也早已全非了。

【English Translation】

A false slip may cause a lifelong regret: the world will no longer be the same as it was when you look back again.

76. 圣贤不白之衷　托之日月

76. Aspirations unable to be expressed by the sages can be entrusted to the sun and moon to declare.

圣贤不白之衷，托之日月；天地不平之气，托之风雷。

【今文解译】　圣贤所未及抒发的胸臆，尽可托付给日月去昭示。
天地间出现的不平之气，尽可托付给风雷去打理。

【English Translation】

All aspirations unable to be expressed by the sages can be entrusted to the sun and moon to declare.
All unfavorable celestial phenomena under heaven can be handed over to the tempest to deal with.

77. 士大夫爱钱　书香化为铜臭

77. When a scholar turns his attention to money, the fragrance of books will become stink of copper coin.

亲兄弟折箸，璧合①翻作瓜分；士大夫爱钱，书香化为铜臭。

【中文注释】　①璧合：由几个部分组成的一套玉雕作品。

【今文解译】　亲兄弟失和，璧合就会四分五裂。
　　　　　　　读书人爱财，书香就会变成铜臭。

【English Translation】

When brothers become estranged, it is just like a full suite of jade artworks recklessly divided up.

When a scholar turns his attention to money, the fragrance of books will become stink of copper coin.

78. 心为形役　尘世马牛

78. Allow your body to labor your mind, and you will be the same as horse or cattle in life.

　　心为形役^①，尘世马牛；身被名牵，樊笼鸡鹜。

【中文注释】　　① 心为形役：心智受役于肉体；肉体拖累心智。

【今文解译】　　如果心灵为肉体所驱使，人就会像牛马一样活在世上。
　　　　　　　　如果人被名声所束缚，就会像鸡鸭一样被关在了笼中。

【English Translation】

Allow your body to labor your mind, and you will be the same as horse or cattle in life.
Get yourself fettered by fame, and you will be the same as a caged chicken or a fenced duck.

79. 留有余智　提防不测

79. Give no full play to your wisdom in order to save some strength to deal with possible unexpected occurrences.

待人而留有余，不尽之恩礼①，可以维系无厌之人心；御事而留有余，不尽之才智，可以提防不测之事变。

【中文注释】　① 恩礼: 恩惠与礼遇。

【今文解译】　与人交往要让别人知道你对他们的恩礼是不会断的, 这样可以维系住永远不知满足的人心。
处理事情要为自己留有余地, 不要才华毕露, 这样可以尽可能地提防不可预测的事情发生。

【English Translation】

Let others know you will do them favors as long as you may, thus you can live in peace with the insatiable among them.
Give no full play to your wisdom in order to save some strength to deal with possible unexpected occurrences.

80. 做事要担当 又要善摆脱

80. In dealing with the world's affairs, one should know when and how to advance and retreat.

　　宇宙内事，要担当，又要善摆脱。不担当，则无经世之事业；不摆脱，则无出世之襟期。

【今文解译】　　世界上的事，一方面要有勇气去担当，另一方面还要有办法去解脱。不去担当，负起社会责任就无从谈起；不会解脱，超然物外的境界就无法达到。

【English Translation】

In dealing with the world's affairs, one should know when and how to advance and retreat: all retreat no advance will fail you to assume your social responsibilities, while all advance no retreat will make it impossible for you to be free from mundaneness.

81. 假认不得真　巧藏不得拙

81. What is false cannot be true; whoever is clever cannot hide his clumsiness.

任他极有见识，看得假认不得真；随你极有聪明，卖得巧藏不得拙。

【今文解译】　不管一个人的见地有多高深，他也许只能识破假象而看不清真相。

不管一个人的脑子有多好使，他也许只会弄巧卖乖而藏不了笨拙。

【English Translation】

No matter how intelligent you are, you may probably penetrate what is false, but may not necessarily ascertain what is true.

No matter how clever you are, you can probably show off your smartness, but can not necessarily hide your clumsiness.

82. 量晴较雨 弄月嘲风

82. It's quite a thing to detect the climatic change or invite friends of yours to enjoy with you the moon and breeze.

种两顷附郭田①，量晴较雨；寻几个知心友，弄月嘲风②。

【中文注释】　① 附郭田: 城市近郊的农田。
② 弄月嘲风: 泛指文人骚客的雅聚, 包括饮酒赋诗, 赏物逗趣, 寻欢作乐。

【今文解译】　在城郊种上两顷地,让它派点预测天气阴晴变化的用场。叫上三五好友来聚聚,大家一起对着明月清风吟诗作赋。

【English Translation】

It's quite a thing to have two hectares of field ploughed near the suburbs to detect the climatic change or three or five bosom friends of yours invited to enjoy with you the moon and breeze.

83. 放下仙佛心　方名为得道

83. Expel the desire for being an immortal-like Buddha, and you will comprehend what the Way is.

　　放得俗人心下，方可为丈夫；放得丈夫心下，方名为仙佛；放得仙佛心下，方名为得道。

【今文解译】　　能将俗人的物质欲望放下，方可做得大丈夫；能将大丈夫的功利心放下，方可称得上是仙佛；能将仙佛的超凡之心放下，方可彻悟道的境界。

【English Translation】

As long as you expel the desire for worldly gains, you can become a true man. As long as you expel the desire for being a true man, you can become an immortal-like Buddha. As long as you expel the desire for being an immortal-like Buddha, you can thoroughly comprehend what the Way is.

84. 执拗者福轻　圆融者禄厚

84. Pigheaded persons have inadequate good fortune while those of mellow character receive affluent emolument.

　　执拗者福轻，而圆融之人其禄必厚；操切者寿夭，而宽厚之士其年必长。故君子不言命①，养性即所以立命②，亦不言天③，尽人④自可以回天。

【中文注释】　　① 不言命: 不谈论命（运）。此处意即不信命。
　　　　　　　　② 养性即所以立命: 通过提高自己的道德修养来安身立命。
　　　　　　　　③ 不言天: 不谈论天（意）。此处意即不信天。
　　　　　　　　④ 尽人: 尽人的力量; 将人的智慧和力量发挥到最大限度。

【今文解译】　　性格固执的人福薄, 而性格圆融的人禄厚; 性格急躁的人寿短, 而性格仁厚的人寿长。所以, 君子从不信命, 而是通过修养心性来安身立命, 也从不信天, 而是依靠发挥自己的力量来战胜一切困难。

【English Translation】

Those who are pigheaded have inadequate good fortune while those of mellow character receive affluent emolument. Those who are impatient in doing anything have a lifespan not as long as it should be, while those who are kind and lenient in social intercourse enjoy longevity. That is why the men of virtue never talk about fate among themselves but would rather get on with their lives by improving their own qualities, and never refer to the topic of God's will but would rather reverse the desperate situations, if any, by relying on their own wisdom and power.

85. 达人撒手悬崖

85. A man well versed in the way of life is he that knows when to rein in at the brink of a precipice.

达人撒手悬崖，俗子沉身苦海。

【今文解译】　能及时悬崖勒马收手不干的人,都是深谙生命之道的人。
为功名利禄不惜在苦海中拼命挣扎的人,都是凡夫俗子。

【English Translation】

A man well versed in the way of life is he that knows when to rein in at the brink of a precipice.
A mean fellow so addressed is he that is deeply submerged by the sea of bitterness.

86. 身世浮名余以梦蝶视之

86. One'd better look at fame and glory with an illusive vision rather than the naked eyes.

身世浮名余以梦蝶视之，断不受肉眼相看。

【今文解译】 一生的名声都只是浮云而已，我会以庄周梦蝶的眼光而非世俗的眼光看待它们。

【English Translation】

To examine the fame and glory gained by myself, I'd like to have it done by resorting to the illusive vision rather than the naked eyes.

87. 百折不回　方能百变不穷

87. Only with a firm will can one find out a foolproof way to deal with various unexpected occurrences.

士人①有百折不回之真心②，才有万变不穷③之妙用。

【中文注释】　① 士人：知识分子，泛指读书人。
② 真心：真正坚强的意志。
③ 万变不穷：变化再多也能应对自如。

【今文解译】　读书人只有具备了百折不挠的精神，才能够从容应对各种变故。

【English Translation】

Only with a firm will undaunted by repeated setbacks can a cultured man find out a foolproof way to deal with various unexpected occurrences.

88. 立业建功　实地着脚

88. Be earnest and down-to-earth if you are determined to establish a competency and make a contribution.

立业建功，事事要从实地着脚①，若少慕声闻②，便成伪果③。

讲道修德，念念要从虚处立基④，若稍计功效⑤，便落尘情⑥。

【中文注释】　① 从实地着脚: 脚踏实地。

② 少慕声闻: 稍微有一点追求虚名的念头。

③ 伪果: 华而不实的结果。

④ 从虚处立基: 此处隐指以不求功利为目的。

⑤ 功效: 成效。喻得失。

⑥ 尘情: 俗套。此处可理解为失败，即修不成正果。

【今文解译】　开创事业，建立功名，其间每一件事都要踏踏实实地做好，来不得半点虚荣，不然就会落个欺世盗名的下场。谈经论道，修身养性，其中每一个念想都要以不求功利为基本出发点，稍有得失方面的计较，就会前功尽弃。

【English Translation】

Those who are determined to establish a competency and make a contribution should do it with earnestness rather than ostentation, otherwise, no effect can be expected thereby.

Those who are lecturing on classics and cultivating virtues should start from where no profit is desirable; any attempt to bother about personal gains or losses might spoil the previous ventures.

89. 兢兢业业心思　潇潇洒洒趣味

89. A man devoted to scholarship should not only have assiduous thoughts in study but also elegant tastes for life.

学者要有段兢业①的心思，又要有段潇洒②的趣味。

【中文注释】　　① 兢业：兢兢业业。
　　　　　　　② 潇洒：洒脱自如。

【今文解译】　　为学者不仅要有刻苦钻研、积极向上的心思，而且还要有
　　　　　　　寄情山水、潇洒开放的趣味。

【English Translation】

A man devoted to scholarship should not only have assiduous thoughts in study but also elegant tastes for life.

90. 无事提防　有事镇定

90. Be on alert when nothing has happened and when something has happened, be calm and collected.

　　无事常如有事时提防，才可以弭意外之变；有事常如无事时镇定，方可以销局中之危。

【今文解译】　　平安无事时要像有事时那样保持警惕，只有这样才能应
　　　　　　　　对突发的变故。
　　　　　　　　有事发生时要像无事时那样保持镇定，唯有如此才能排
　　　　　　　　除面临的危险。

【English Translation】

When nothing has happened, one should be on alert as if something is going to happen, so that one can cope well with the situation unexpected.

When something has happened, one should be calm and collected as if nothing had happened, so that one can do away with the danger confronted.

91. 穷通之境未遭　主持之局已定

91. Plan the layout of personal development prior to the coming of tough time or prosperity.

　　穷通之境未遭，主持之局已定；老病之势未催，生死之关先破。求之今人，谁堪语此？

【今文解译】　在未遇到穷困或显达之前，人就应该预先将自己的个人发展问题完成布局；还未受到衰老和疾病的折磨之前，人就应该提前把生死问题看个透。当今世界，我可以和谁谈论这些问题呢？

【English Translation】

Plan the layout of personal development prior to the coming of tough time or prosperity. Penetrate the issue of life and death prior to suffering the ravages of being old and sick. Seeking among today's masses, is there anyone whom I can discuss the subjects with?

92. 枝头秋叶　檐前野鸟

92. Not be the autumn leaves hanging on the branches or the caged birds under the eaves.

　　枝头秋叶，将落犹然恋树；檐前野鸟，除死方得离笼。人之处世，可怜如此。

【今文解译】　　秋叶已经枯黄，将要飘落却还依恋着树枝不肯离去；寄居檐前的野鸟，只有等到断了气才能脱离牢笼。人的境遇若此，岂不凄惨？！

【English Translation】

The autumn leaves hanging on the branches are reluctant to part with the trees even when they are to fall. The wild birds kept under the eaves cannot extricate themselves from the cages until they breathe their last. Human beings, if getting on like this, are really pitiful!

93. 刚强终不胜柔弱

93. The hard are no match for the supple in the end.

舌存，常见齿亡；刚强，终不胜柔弱。户朽，未闻枢蠹；偏执，岂及乎圆融^①。

【中文注释】 　① 圆融: 灵活变通; 机灵; 圆滑。

【今文解译】 　牙齿掉光了, 可舌头还完好无损, 可见刚强终难胜过柔弱。
门板腐朽了, 可门轴却未遭虫蛀, 可见偏执总比不上圆融。

【English Translation】

It always follows that the tongue will remain intact even though all the teeth are gone. From this we know that the hard are no match for the supple in the end.

It always follows that the door-hinge will never develop moths even though the door is rotten. From this we know that being inflexible and rigid is not as good as being flexible and accommodating.

94. 声应气求之夫　风行水上之文

94. Good friendship depends on mutual understandings; good writings are like the wind skimming over the water.

声应气求之夫，决不在于寻行数墨之士；风行水上之文，决不在于一句一字之奇。

【今文解译】　志趣相投的挚友，无须借助往来文牍增进彼此的了解。
如行云流水般上佳的文章，决不在于一字一句的奇妙。

【English Translation】

Congenial friends do not need exchange of correspondence to maintain the mutual understandings between them.
Writings as fluent as the wind skimming over the water are not dependent on the splendor of a single sentence or word.

95. 才智英敏者　宜以学问摄其躁

95. The man of ability and intelligence should harmonize his impetuous disposition with acquired knowledge.

才智英敏①者，宜以学问摄其躁②；气节激昂③者，当以德性融其偏④。

【中文注释】　①才智英敏：才华和智慧皆出色过人。

②以学问摄其躁：用所学的知识调理浮躁的气性。

③气节激昂：动不动就义愤填膺，慷慨激昂。

④以德性融其偏：用提高自己的修为消除偏激倾向。

【今文解译】　才智英敏的人，应该用所学的知识来调理自己的浮躁情绪。

气节激昂的人，应该通过道德修养来消除自己的偏激倾向。

【English Translation】

He who is excellent in ability and intelligence should harmonize his impetuous temperament with acquired knowledge.

He who easily demonstrates his moral indignation at every turn should melt his extreme disposition through self-cultivation.

96. 身居轩冕之中　须有山林气味

96. Those who enjoy high positions and handsome salaries should not be dispensed of the plain makings of a hermit.

居轩冕之中①，要有山林的气味②；处林泉之下，常怀廊庙③的经纶④。

【中文注释】　① 居轩冕之中：轩冕，古代卿大夫的轩车和冕服。居轩冕之中，喻身居高位、俸禄丰厚的官员。
② 山林的气味：山林，与此后的"林泉"二字同义，喻指与世无争；气味，气息。山林的气味，可理解为与世无争的意趣或情调。
③ 廊庙：朝廷。此处表示治国安邦的意思。
④ 经纶：本意为经过整理的蚕丝。此处喻规划、管理政治的才能。结合前面的"廊庙"二字，可理解为"治国安邦的抱负和才能"。

【今文解译】　身居要职的，不可没有山林居士那种淡泊名利的闲情逸致。
以林泉为伴的，不可没有胸怀天下、经济国家社稷的才志。

【English Translation】

Those who enjoy high positions and handsome salaries should not be dispensed of the plain makings of a hermit in mountains and forests.
Those who live in seclusion far from the earthly world must be always provided with ambitions and talents to serve the country and people.

97. 少言语以当贵　多著述以当富

97. Take it as acquiring dignity to speak less and as gaining wealth to write aplenty.

少言语以当贵，多著述以当富，载清名以当车，咀英华以当肉。

【今文解译】　把少说话当作是尊贵，把多著书当作是富有，把获得好名声当作是驾车，把品读经典当作是吃肉。

【 English Translation 】

Take it as acquiring dignity to speak less.
Take it as gaining wealth to write aplenty.
Take it as driving a chariot to carry a good reputation.
Take it as chewing meat to make a scrutiny of classics.

98. 要做男子　须负刚肠

98. One who wants to be a real man should be of iron-will and stoneheartedness.

要做男子，须负刚肠；欲学古人，当坚苦志。

【今文解译】　要做大丈夫，必须具备铁石般刚硬的心肠。
要学古仿贤，必须磨炼和坚定自己的意志。

【English Translation】

One who wants to be a real man should be of iron-will and stoneheartedness. One who intends to imitate the ancient sages should be steadfast and assiduous.

99. 柔玉温香　可成白骨

99. Women, even with jade-like skin and fragrant flesh, will finally become white bones.

　　荷钱榆荚①，飞来都作青蚨②；柔玉温香③，观想可成白骨。

【中文注释】　　① 荷钱榆荚：荷钱，荷叶初生时，形小如钱，故称荷钱；榆荚，榆树尚未长叶时，枝间先生榆荚，色白，形状似钱，故称榆钱。
② 青蚨：原是《搜神记》中记载的一种会飞的虫子，此处借指铜钱。
③ 柔玉温香：指美丽的女子。

【今文解译】　　荷叶榆荚，飞到眼前尽可当作铜钱。
柔玉温香，才想说艳羡就已成白骨。

【English Translation】

Lotus leaflets and elm seedlings*, when blown to us by the wind, may all be taken as real copper coins in use.
Women, even with jade-like skin and fragrant flesh, will become white bones the minute we are to admire.

100. 空烦恼场　绝营求念

100. Banish the vexing thoughts, abandon the desire for fame and gain, and you will enjoy ease and liberty.

烦恼场空，身住清凉世界①；营求念绝，心归自在乾坤。

【中文注释】　①清凉世界：佛家所说的去除了身心烦恼的世界。

【今文解译】　抛却了尘世间的一切烦恼，身体也就进入了清凉的世界。
放弃了追名逐利的念头，心也就回到了自由自在的境地。

【English Translation】

So long as you banish from your mind the vexing thoughts, you will feel as if your body were in a world brimming with cool and refreshing air.
So long as you abandon the desire for fame and gain, you will feel as if your heart had returned to the realm of splendor and liberty.

101. 闲随老衲清谭 戏与骚人白战

101. When not occupied, it's quite a joy to chat with an old monk and a fun to chant with a poet.

斜阳树下，闲随老衲^①清谭^②；深雪^③堂中，戏与骚人^④白战^⑤。

【中文注释】　① 老衲: 老和尚。
　　　　　　　② 清谭: 清谈。纯粹的聊天, 闲聊。
　　　　　　　③ 深雪: 此处指大雪天。
　　　　　　　④ 骚人: 泛指文人墨客, 此处指诗人。
　　　　　　　⑤ 白战: 用诗文对吟对唱, 禁用某些常用的字眼。

【今文解译】　夕阳西照, 我与老僧悠闲地在树下清谈。
　　　　　　　积雪甚深, 我与诗人在厅堂中对诗比赋。

【 English Translation 】

How leisurely the moment is when the old monk and I are sitting under a tree with a slanting sun in the west, chatting as we will!
How joyful the occasion is when the poet and I stay indoors at a heavy-snowy day, chanting playfully the poems with a moody tune!

102. 宁为真士夫　不为假道学

102. Rather be an honest Confucian scholar than a sanctimonious Taoist follower.

宁为真士夫①，不为假道学②；宁为兰摧玉折，不作萧敷艾荣③。

【中文注释】　① 士夫：士大夫。此处指儒学者。
② 假道学：伪善的道学者；表面上正经、实际上很坏的人；伪君子。
③ 萧敷艾荣：萧、艾，蒿草；敷、荣，茂盛状。萧敷艾荣，指蒿草长得很茂盛或长得很茂盛的蒿草。常喻才能低下、品行卑劣的人得势于一时。

【今文解译】　宁可做一个实心实意的儒家学者，也不做伪善的假道学先生。
宁可做凋谢的兰花和破碎的美玉，也不做长得很茂盛的萧艾。

【English Translation】

Rather be an honest Confucian scholar than a sanctimonious Taoist follower.
Rather be a wrecked orchid or a broken jade than luxuriant field grasses.

103. 觑破兴衰究竟　人我得失冰消

103. A perception of the outcomes in rise and fall helps people to give up their thoughts to personal gains and losses.

觑破兴衰究竟①，人我②得失冰消；阅尽寂寞繁华③，豪杰心肠灰冷④。

【中文注释】　① 究竟: 透彻; 彻彻底底的真相。
② 人我: 我们大家; 人人; 每个人。
③ 寂寞繁华: 落寞与奢华。
④ 心肠灰冷: 比喻争强好胜的心不再那么激烈。

【今文解译】　看透了人世间的兴盛衰亡, 人与人之间的患得患失现象就会像冰块一样消融。
阅尽了人世间的寂寞繁华, 英雄豪杰争强好胜的心就会像死灰一般冷却下来。

【English Translation】

Having perceived the outcomes in rise and fall would help people to avoid being too particular about their personal gains and losses.
Having experienced both desolation and prosperity would help the heroic to cool off their fervent desires to win over each other.

104. 名山乏侣　不解壁上芒鞋

104. Outing to a mountainous resort with no good company coming along is not as desirable as staying at home.

名山乏侣，不解壁上芒鞋；好景无诗，虚怀囊中锦字。

【今文解译】　游历名山没有好的旅伴一起同行，还不如呆在家里，让草鞋静静地挂在墙上。

面对秀丽景色但却无诗助兴，即使是才高八斗，学富五车，终究是浪得虚名。

【English Translation】

Outing to a mountainous resort with no good company coming along is not as desirable as staying at home and letting the straw sandals hung on the wall untouched.

Failing to write a verse to liven things up to the beautiful scene within sight, how can a literary man who is wealthy in knowledge be worthy of what he has learned?

105. 无技最苦　多技最劳

105. Those with no skill are most hardworking and utterly exhausted, those with multiple skills.

是技皆可成名天下，惟无技之人最苦；片技即足以自立天下，惟多技之人最劳。

【今文解译】　有技能就不怕吃不开,只有没有技能的人才活得最辛苦。
　　　　　　有一技之长就能立足社会,而掌握多种技能的人最操劳。

【English Translation】

One who possesses a skill will get known to the public at last, while those with no skill have to consume their physical strength by laboring in an extremely difficult situation.

Talent in one aspect or another is quite enough for one to earn a living by oneself, while those who are talented in many aspects are bound to live in a state of utter exhaustion.

106. 才士不妨泛驾　诤臣岂合模棱

106. A man of talent may well roam the world at will, but a court official in submitting admonitions is not allowed to speak in an equivocal way.

着履登山，翠微中独逢老衲；乘桴浮海，雪浪里群傍闲鸥。才士不妨泛驾，辕下驹吾弗愿也；诤臣①岂合模棱，殿上虎君无尤焉。

【中文注释】　① 诤臣：敢于直言规劝国君缺失的臣子。

【今文解译】　脚穿草鞋独自去登山，许于青翠的山色间遇见一位老僧。驾着筏子漂浮在海上，白浪里定有成群的海鸥在天上伴飞。才子不妨云游天下，怎甘心做拉套拖车的辕马？诤臣贵在敢于直言，哪怕大殿之上坐着如虎一般的君王。

【English Translation】

Ascending alone the mountains in straw sandals, one is likely to meet an old monk amidst the verdant.

Drifting in raft on the wavy sea, one is bound to be accompanied by the seagulls in crowd.

It is well enough for a man of talent to roam the world at will. How can he be a horse between the shafts?

A court official daring to submit admonitions, not allowed to speak in an equivocal way, should always make upright statements even in the presence of a tiger-like sovereign.

107. 宁为薄幸狂夫 不作厚颜君子

107. Rather be a frivolous maniac than a shameless hypocrite.

　　吟诗劣于讲书，骂座恶于足恭。两而揆之，宁为薄幸狂夫，不作厚颜君子。

【今文解译】 　　吟诗的不如讲书的那么有严肃稳重，但直抒胸臆；酒席上的破口漫骂要比待人过于毕恭毕敬更加恶劣，但快意恩仇。如果非要在二者之间做选择，我宁愿做个轻薄的狂徒，也不做厚颜无耻的伪君子。

【English Translation】

Reciting verses is no better than lecturing on classics. Making drunken scenes is no better than showing modesty out of sense. But if a choice must be made between the twos, the answer would be as follows: rather be a frivolous maniac than a shameless hypocrite.

108. 魑魅满前　笑著阮家无鬼论

108. When everywhere are seen the ones who appear as sinister as the ghosts, I can't help pouring ridicule on the viewpoint of non-existence of ghosts.

　　魑魅满前，笑著阮家无鬼论①；炎嚣阅世②，愁披刘氏北风图③，气夺山川，色结烟霞④。

【中文注释】　① 阮家无鬼论: 阮家，即阮瞻，"竹林七贤"之一阮咸之子，平素坚持无鬼论。
　　　　　　　② 炎嚣阅世: 物欲甚嚣尘上的世界。
　　　　　　　③ 刘氏北风图: 刘氏，刘褒，汉代画家，曾画《北风图》一幅，其中意趣深远，笔墨精炼，人们看了都觉得十分凉爽。
　　　　　　　④ 气夺山川，色结烟霞: 气势盖过了山川的雄伟，墨色凝聚着烟霞的炫彩。

【今文解译】　到处是鬼魅一样的人在眼前晃荡，因而忍不住嘲笑起阮瞻的无鬼论来。看着满世界追名逐利的人，心中不由得想起刘褒的《北风图》来，那叫一个气夺山川，色结烟霞。

【English Translation】

When everywhere are seen the ones who appear as sinister as the ghosts, I can't help pouring ridicule on Ruan Zan*'s viewpoint of non-existence of ghosts.

The world is brimming with human desires for material gains, and so reminds me of Liu Bao*'s masterpiece *Picture of the North Wind*, which is coated with a dreadful hue of power and grandeur, and colored in mist and haze.

【English Annotation】

* Ruan Zan: An official of the Western Jin Dynasty, who died young between 307 and 312, well known for his viewpoint of non-existence of ghosts.

* Liu Bao: An official good at painting at the reign of Emperor Huan (147-167) of the Eastern Han Dynasty. *Picture of the North Wind* is his most famous masterpiece which was said that one would feel very cool by looking at this picture.

109. 至音不合众　至宝不同众好

109. Music played to its extreme is hard for all to appreciate; treasures of the supreme class are difficult for all to appraise.

至音不合众听，故伯牙绝弦①；至宝不同众好，故卞和泣玉②。

【中文注释】　① 伯牙绝弦：伯牙，春秋时楚国琴师，他所演奏的《高山流水》只有钟子期能听懂。钟子期死后，伯牙失去唯一的知音，伤心之下毁掉了自己的琴，余生不再弹琴。
② 卞和泣玉：卞和，战国时楚国人，将一块偶得的璞玉相继献给楚厉王和楚武王，二王不仅不识玉，反而还认为他欺君，分别剁去他的左右脚。卞和为玉不被赏识而在荆山下痛哭，后楚文王让人将其琢磨出美玉，遂称和氏璧。

【今文解译】　格调高雅的音乐并非一般人所能欣赏，所以伯牙毁掉了自己的琴。
最珍贵的宝物普通的人不知其价值，所以卞和才为他的璞玉哭泣。

【English Translation】

Highbrow music played to its extreme is difficult for all to appreciate, so Bo Ya* smashed his *qin**.
Valuable treasures of the supreme class are difficult for all to appraise, so Bian He* wailed for his jade.

【English Annotation】

* Bo Ya: A famous fiddler of the state of Chu during the Spring and Autumn Period (770BC-476BC). Once, Bo Ya was playing the *qin* (see the following note. — tr.) and Zhong Ziqi was appreciating the music. At first, Bo Ya was pining for lofty mountains. Zhong Ziqi said, "Wonderful music! It is as majestic as lofty mountains." After a while Bo Ya was pining for running water. Zhong Ziqi again said, "Wonderful music! Its flowing rhythm jingles

just like running water." After Zhong Ziqi died, Bo Ya smashed his *qin*, broke its strings and never played it again in the rest of his life, as he believed that no one in the world understood his music but Zhong Ziqi.

* *qin*: A traditional Chinese musical instrument with seven or five strings, rather like the zither.

* Bian He: A native of the state of Chu during the Warring States Period (475BC-221BC), who tried to present an uncut jade to King Li and then to King Wu after refused by the former, but with no knowledge about the value of the jade, the two kings, instead of accepting it, thought Bian He was practicing deception on them and therefore cut his feet in succession. Bian He was sad and wailed at the foot of the Jingshan Mountain where he accidentally got this jade. After the death of King Wu, King Wen, the successor, upon hearing the story, ordered jade craftsmen to cut open the stone. They discovered a piece of precious jade which was thereupon named "The Jade of He's".

110. 世人白昼寐语

110. People love to repeat at daytime what they talked about in dreams.

世人白昼寐语，苟能于寐中作白昼语，可谓常惺惺矣。

【今文解译】 世人总喜欢在大白天里复述梦里说过的话，但是如果有人能在梦里复述大白天里说过的话，那么这个人可以说是能常常保持清醒的了。

【English Translation】

People love to repeat at daytime what they talked about in dreams. But if there is someone who could repeat in his sleep what he talked about in broad daylight, he must be the one who is really above the common consciousness.

111. 拨开世上尘氛　消却心中鄙吝

111. Turn away the turmoil and confusion from without and expel the sordidness and stinginess from within.

　　拨开世上尘氛，胸中自无火炎冰竞；消却心中鄙吝，眼前时有月到风来。

【今文解译】　能够将外界的各种纷扰撇开不顾，心中自然就不会有火烧般的焦灼和如履薄冰般的胆战心惊。

能够将自己内心那些卑鄙吝啬的东西清除干净，自然就会感觉到时不时有清风明月来光顾你。

【English Translation】

Turn away the turmoil and confusion from without, and one will be mentally freed from concern as if facing fire and fear as if walking on the thin ice.

Expel the sordidness and stinginess from within, and one will naturally feel as if the bright moon and gentle breeze would come around from time to time.

112. 才子安心草舍　佳人适意蓬门

112. A talented scholar is he who is willing to reside in a thatched hut; a virtuous beauty is she who is content to be the daughter-in-law of a humble family.

才子安心草舍者，足登玉堂；佳人适意蓬门者，堪贮金屋。

【今文解译】　能安心居住在茅草屋里的才子，一定足可登上大雅之堂。
　　　　　　　能适意嫁入寒门的佳人，一定有资格住进为她盖的金屋。

【English Translation】

A talented scholar willing to reside in a thatched hut is entitled to have his presence in a sumptuous hall.

A beauty content to be the daughter-in-law of a humble family is worthy to be housed in a golden mansion.

113. 喜传语者　不可与语

113. Do not speak your mind to those who are keenly fond of gossip.

喜传语者，不可与语；好议事者，不可图事。

【今文解译】　切不可对喜欢飞短流长的人说出你心里话。
切不可与有事就好说长道短的人共谋一事。

【 English Translation 】

Do not speak your mind to those who are keenly fond of gossip.
Do not plan matters with those who easily speak at great length.

114. 不留昨日之非　不执今日之是

114. What was wrong yesterday should not be retained; what is correct today may not be held too fast.

　　昨日之非不可留，留之则根烬复萌，而尘情终累乎理趣。今日之是不可执，执之则渣滓未化，而理趣反转为欲根。

【今文解译】　昨天错误的东西不应该留着，留着会有死灰复燃的可能，因为人的凡心俗情终究会影响到义理情趣。
今天正确的东西不可太执着，太执着了，似是而非的部分就有可能使人的义理情趣变成欲望的温床。

【English Translation】

What was wrong yesterday should not be retained, or the burnt root of it will revive itself and thereby enable the vulgar interests to tie down your aspiration and taste.

What is correct today may not be held too fast, or the parts superficially correct but actually wrong in it will possibly turn your aspiration and taste into a hotbed of desires.

115. 炫奇之疾　医以平易

115. To be unassuming and amiable is a remedy for the flaw in resorting to novelty.

炫奇之疾，医以平易；英发之疾，医以深沉；阔大之疾，医以充实。

【今文解译】　炫耀奇异的毛病，要用平易之法来医治。
夸夸其谈的毛病，要用深沉之法来医治。
喜欢虚头巴脑的毛病，要用厚重之法来医治。

【English Translation】

To be unassuming and amiable is a remedy for the flaw in resorting to novelty.
To keep the depth in thinking is a remedy for the flaw in talking big.
To elevate inner power is a remedy for the flaw in keeping up appearances.

116. 人常想病时　则尘心便减

116. Frequently reflect on the hard time of being ill, and one will moderate his desire for material gains.

人常想病时，则尘心便减；人常想死时，则道念自生。

【今文解译】　只有当人们把生病的痛苦常记于心时，追求名利的心思才会消减。
只有当人们把死当作必然归宿常记于心时，对生的意义才会彻悟。

【English Translation】

Only when a man frequently reflects on the hard time of being ill, can he keep his desire for material gains in moderation.
Only when a man frequently bears in mind that death is but a matter of homecoming, can he gain a thorough understanding of life.

117. 恩爱吾之仇也

117. The affair of man and woman is my enemy.

恩爱吾之仇也，富贵身之累也。

【今文解译】　正如男女之情是我的仇敌，富贵荣华是我身心的拖累。

【English Translation】

Just as the affair of man and woman is my enemy, so the accumulation of wealth and glory is my burden.

118. 人生善读书　享世间清福

118. The person who has books and time to read enjoys leisurely happiness in life.

　　人生有书可读，有暇得读，有资能读，又涵养之如不识字人，是谓善读书者。享世间清福，未有过于此也。

【今文解译】　有书可读，有时间读书，有钱可资读书，读了书后又不失目不识丁者那种淳朴与敦厚，这样的人才是最适合读书的。人世间所谓的清福不过如此。

【English Translation】

The person most suitable for reading is one who has books to read, enough time and money to spend on reading, and at the same time whose makings remain as pure and honest as an illiterate person. Has there ever been any happiness in the world as leisurely as such?

119. 古人不掩瑕瑜　今人难知真伪

119. The ancients never concealed their defects while the moderns are like antiques you can never tell real from false.

　　古之人，如陈玉石于市肆，瑕瑜不掩；今之人，如货古玩于时贾，真伪难知。

【今文解译】　古时候的人就像摆在集市上的璞玉一样，毫不掩饰地将自己的优点和缺点都展现在世人面前；而当今的人们却像顾主兜售给古玩店的古玩一样，真伪难以辨别。

【English Translation】

The ancient people were like jades in the fair, with their defects and merits not concealed; while the modern people are like the antiques peddled to antique stores, about which, no one can tell the real from the false.

120. 以忍制己情　以恕制人情

120. Restrain the desires of our own and tolerate the inveterate habits of others.

　　己情不可纵，当用逆之法制之，其道在一忍①字。人情不可拂，当用顺之法制之，其道在一恕②字。

【中文注释】　①忍：忍耐。
　　　　　　　②恕：宽容；包涵；包容。

【今文解译】　自己的欲念不可放纵，而应当加以克制，唯一有效的方法就是"忍"。
　　　　　　　世人的痼习不要拂逆，而应当因势利导，唯一可行的方法就是"恕"。

【English Translation】

Our personal desires should not be indulged, but should be restrained; to achieve which forbearance is the very word to stick to.

The habits of the world should not be opposed, but should be guided by circumstances; to make the best of which tolerance is the very word to stick to.

121. 随遇而安　何不清闲

121. A leisurely life will be assured if one can adapt himself to the circumstances.

人言天不禁人富贵，而禁人清闲，人自不闲耳。若能随遇而安，不图将来，不追既往，不蔽目前，何不清闲之有？

【今文解译】　都说老天不禁止人们去追求荣华富贵，但却禁止人们闲着不干事，所以大家都忙得不亦乐乎。若能做到随遇而安，不为将来处心积虑，不再追悔既往，不被眼前的事物所蒙蔽，何愁不得清闲？

【English Translation】

It is said that Heaven never prohibits people from becoming rich and honorable, but prohibits them from becoming lazy and idle. That's why people get themselves fully occupied. If they can accommodate themselves to the circumstances, do not take the pains to anticipate the future, nor repent the past, nor be perplexed by the things confronted, how can they fail to find a good time for themselves, free and easy?

122. 浮云有常情　流水多浓旨

122. Floating clouds are more understandable than human affairs and running waters more affectionate than human feelings.

观世态之极幻，则浮云转有常情；咀世味之昏空，则流水翻多浓旨。

【今文解译】　世态炎凉的变化速度之快实在无法预测，倒是天上浮云的变化更有规律可循。
　　　　　　　人情世故淡寡冷漠，倒是江河湖海里的滚滚流水更能给人以耐人寻味的温情。

【 English Translation 】

Observe the inconstant changes of the way of the world, and one will find that the floating clouds are even more understandable than human affairs.
Ponder on the thinness of public morals and mores, and one will find that the running waters are even more affectionate than human feelings.

123. 贫士肯济人　闹场能笃学

123. A poor scholar who is ready to lend a helping hand can concentrate on study in the hubbub.

贫士①肯济人，才是性天②中惠泽③；闹场④能笃学⑤，方为心地上工夫。

【中文注释】　① 贫士：寒士；穷人。

② 性天：天性；本性；内心。

③ 惠泽：此处喻仁慈、仁厚。

④ 闹场：吵吵闹闹的环境；喧嚣声中。

⑤ 笃学：专心于读书学习。

【今文解译】　生活贫寒的人肯解囊接济别人，才是真正发自内心的仁慈。

能在喧闹嘈杂的地方专心读书，才是真正立志为学的功夫。

【English Translation】

A poor scholar who is ready to help others at any moment must be the one who is merciful by nature.

He who can concentrate on study in a noisy circumstance must be the one who has really made his mind to.

124. 了心自了事　逃世应逃名

124. To eliminate a concern is to bring an end to the thing concerned; to renounce the world is to expel the desire for fame from within.

了心自了事，犹根拔而草不生；逃世不逃名，似膻存而蚋还集。

【今文解译】　了结事情才能了却心中的挂虑，这就好比拔掉了根才算真正铲除了杂草。

远离尘嚣但心里却还惦记着名声，这就好比腥膻之物不除还会招来虫蝇。

【English Translation】

To eliminate a concern is to bring an end to the thing concerned. It is just the same as to eradicate weeds once and for all is to pull up the roots.

Renouncing the world but still longing for the earthly fame is similar to driving away the insects by retaining the rancid matters before them.

125. 风流得意　鬼胜顽仙

125. An unconventional talented ghost prevails over a stubborn immortal.

风流得意，则才鬼独胜顽仙；孽债为烦，则芳魂毒于虐祟。

【今文解译】　风流倜傥而自鸣得意，即使是稍有才气的鬼魅也远远胜过冥顽不灵的神仙。

因为孽债而烦恼缠身，即使是美丽女子的阴魂也比凶神恶煞的鬼神要暴戾。

【English Translation】

A talented ghost, if provided with unconventional and self-satisfied temperament, can prevail over a stubborn immortal.

The spirit of a dead female beauty, if troubled by sinful degradation and sentiments, is more ferocious than a cruel demon.

126. 不因人言而悟　不因外境而得

126. Realization obtained through others' reminding and interest aroused by exterior causes are always not constant.

事理因人言而悟者，有悟还有迷，总不如自悟之了了；意兴从外境而得者，有得还有失，总不如自得之休休。

【今文解译】　事物中所含的道理通过别人的提醒才明白，不免会时而清楚时而迷糊，总不如自己搞明白的那么了然于心。
由外界因素而促发的意趣和兴味，不免会有时有时无的感觉，总不如发自内心的意趣和兴味那么持久耐享。

【English Translation】

The reason in a thing understood through others' reminding is now clear then not clear, and is therefore naturally inferior to what perceived by oneself.
The interest in doing a thing aroused by exterior causes is now existent then nonexistent, and is therefore naturally not as durable as the pleasure heartfelt.

127. 简淡出豪杰　忠孝成神仙

127. To be a hero, one should start with ordinariness; to be a deity, one should start with loyalty and filialness.

豪杰向简淡中求，神仙从忠孝上起。

【今文解译】　当英雄豪杰要从平凡做起。
　　　　　　　想成为神仙要从忠孝做起。

【English Translation】

To be a man as the true heroes one should start with simplicity and plainness.
To be a man as the immortals one should start with loyalty and filialness.

128. 浇花种树　道人魔障

128. The hobby to water flowers and plant trees is at last a barrier in the heart set by a monster.

招客留宾，为欢可喜，未断尘世之攀援；浇花种树，嗜好虽清，亦是道人之魔障①。

【中文注释】　① 魔障：佛家用语。恶魔在人们心中所设的障碍。

【今文解译】　招待宾客，为的是欢聚一堂，却还是有攀附权贵、拉帮结派的嫌疑。
浇花种树，嗜好虽然清闲高雅，毕竟也还是修道之人心里的魔障。

【English Translation】

It's a pleasure for the host to entertain friends and detain guests, but such a doing also shows that he has the attempt to play up to those of power and influence.
It's a nice hobby to water flowers and plant trees, but to a person bent on self-cultivation, such an activity also looks like a barrier in the heart set by a monster.

129. 天下之灵　千古如新

129. The spirit of the world will remain as ever fresh as it has been.

灵天下有一言之微，而千古如新。一字之义，而百世如见者，安可泯灭之？故风、雷、雨、露，天之灵；山、川、民、物，地之灵；语、言、文、字，人之灵。此三才之用，无非一灵以神其间，而又何可泯灭之？

【今文解译】　天下万事万物都是有灵的。由于有了灵，一句微不足道的话，可以历经千年而新意如故；一个字的含义，可以流传百代而依然读之有物。这样有生命力的字句怎可泯灭呢？！风雷雨露是天的灵，山川民物是地的灵，语言文字是人的灵。天、地、人三才之所以有这许多现象，无一不是灵在其中尽显神奇，又怎么可以让灵泯灭了呢？！

【English Translation】

In this world of spirit, even a most inconsiderable remark uttered by a nobody can remain as fresh as it was thousands of years prior. How can the significance of a word eyewitnessed throughout the ages be eliminated?

The winds, thunders, rains and dews are the spirit of heaven. The mountains, rivers, living beings and products are the spirit of earth. The language, speech, writings and words are the spirit of humans. Any performance of the three is just the miraculous presence or power of a relevant spirit. How can they be eliminated?

130. 人生有三乐　阅经会友云游

130. Reading Buddhist scriptures, entertaining friends and outing to roam the world are the three great pleasures in life.

闭门阅佛书，开门接佳客，出门寻山水。此人生三乐。

【今文解译】　　关起门来阅读佛家经卷，开门迎接嘉宾莅临，出门去游历山川美景。这是人生三大乐事。

【English Translation】

Shut yourself up and bend on reading Buddhist scriptures; open the house to entertain your distinguished friends; out to have a journey to the mountains and rivers. These are the three joys of life.

131. 眼里无点灰尘　方可读书千卷

131. Only by keeping your eyes away from dust can you read a thousand books as you will.

眼里无点灰尘，方可读书千卷；胸中没些渣滓，才能处世一番。

【今文解译】　眼里没有灰尘，方可阅尽书籍千卷。
心里少些成见，才能与人相安无事。

【English Translation】

Only by keeping your eyes away from dust can you read a thousand books as you will.

Only by renouncing the prejudices in your mind can you deal with the world properly.

132. 不作风波于世上

132. One won't be worried if one does nothing to trouble the world.

不作风波^①于世上，自无冰炭^②到胸中。

【中文注释】　① 风波：兴风作浪。此处作制造麻烦之意解更为妥切。
　　　　　　　② 冰炭：忽冷忽热之意。隐指忐忑不安的焦躁情绪。

【今文解译】　不为一己之私给世界制造麻烦，心里自然无须忐忑不安。

【English Translation】

One won't be worried if one does nothing to trouble the world for the sake of one's own desires.

133. 无事不乐而忧　是一座活地狱

133. Worrying while nothing has happened makes people live in hell.

无事而忧，对景不乐，即自家亦不知是何缘故。这便是一座活地狱①，更说什么铜床铁柱、剑树刀山也。

【中文注释】　① 活地狱：地狱是佛教传说中人死后灵魂受折磨的地方，后面出现的"铜床铁柱"和"剑树刀山"都是地狱里折磨人的刑具。活地狱意指人活着的时候所受的罪罚，具有"现世报"和"活受罪"的含意。

【今文解译】　无事相扰却忧心忡忡，对着美景却闷闷不乐，连自己都不知道这究竟是何缘故。其实这就是佛教所说的活地狱，且不说真地狱里那些可怕的铜床铁柱和剑树刀山了。

【English Translation】

That a man entertains fears when nothing has happened, remains in low spirits when facing a beautiful scene, and at the same time does not know the reason why things are like this, amounts to living a hell-like life, though not as horrible as the scalding-bronze beds, burning-iron poles, trees of swords and mountains of knives in the real hell*.

【English Annotation】

* The real hell: As some Chinese legends have it, hell, based on Buddhism concept of Naraka, is an underground maze with 18 levels and various chambers in which one must pay for the sins of their life. The scalding-bronze beds, burning-iron poles, trees of swords and mountains of knives mentioned in the text are the tortures included in the list of punishment.

134. 必出世者　方能入世

134. Before traveling in the mundane world one must first make up his mind to transcend it.

必出世①者，方能入世②，不则世缘③易堕；必入世者，方能出世，不则空趣④难持。

【中文注释】　① 出世：佛教常用语。脱离尘世的束缚、超越尘世或摆脱俗世的诱惑等。
② 入世：佛教常用语。经历并接受俗世各种诱惑的挑战和考验。
③ 世缘：世间的影响和诱惑。
④ 空趣：空，是指缘起无自性，简单说是指事物任何时候必须依赖各种因缘才能存在，而不是一般自然观念里能够独立存在；趣，指信念。空趣，即对虚空的信念。

【今文解译】　只有抱定必出世信念的人才能入世，不然就容易受世俗影响而堕落。
只有充分做好必入世准备的人才能出世，不然保持空趣就是一句空话。

【English Translation】

Before traveling in the mundane world one must first make up one's mind to transcend it, otherwise one will be corrupted by the vanity of the time.
Before transcending the mundane world one must first get ready to have a wild travel in it, otherwise one will lose conviction in the realm of phantoms.

135. 人有一字不识而多诗意

135. There are people who can't read a word and yet can give utterances full of poetic flavor.

人有一字不识而多诗意，一偈不参^①而多禅意^②，一勺不濡而多酒意^③，一石不晓而多画意^④。淡宕^⑤故也。

【中文注释】　① 一偈不参：偈，即佛偈，类似于世俗中的名言警句。一偈不参意为从来不参悟佛偈。

② 多禅意：禅意，佛教术语。犹禅心，指清空安宁的心。多禅意也即对禅意很熟悉。

③ 酒意：喝酒的乐趣。

④ 多画意：对如何作画很有想法。此处因为要与"一石不晓"相呼应，所以宜转意理解成"艺术感十足"或"充满艺术灵感"。

⑤ 淡宕：又作"淡荡"，淡泊而无拘无束。

【今文解译】　有些人一字不识但说起话来诗意盎然，一句佛偈都不参但深谙禅机，一滴酒不沾但深知杯中之物给人带来的乐趣，对奇石一窍不通但艺术感十足。这都因为他们有一个淡泊而不受拘束的性格。

【English Translation】

There are some people who can't read a word and yet can give utterances full of poetic flavor, some people who never meditate on the librettos in Buddhist scripture and yet can penetrate the allegorical words and gestures used by Chan monks, some people who never drink wine and yet can tell the taste in cups, and some people who do not know anything about wonder stones and yet have a good sense of art. All these are attributed to their pure temperament and indulgent imagination.

136. 眉上几分愁　且去观棋酌酒

136. When you are in bad mood, go and watch a chess game, or go and have a sip.

眉上几分愁，且去观棋酌酒；心中多少乐，只来种竹浇花。

【今文解译】　愁眉不展时，不妨去观观棋喝喝酒。
　　　　　　　心情舒坦时，不妨去种种竹浇浇花。

【English Translation】

When you are in bad mood, go and watch a chess game, or go and have a sip.
When you are in good mood, go and plant bamboos, or go and water flowers.

137. 得心上本来　方可言了心

137. Only when recognizing the character of one's own nature can one understand the essence of one's own heart.

完得心上之本来，方可言了心；尽得世间之常道，才堪论出世。

【今文解译】　只有彻底认识到自己的天性，才有可能了解自己心的本质。

只有彻悟通行世间的常理，才可谈论如何脱离尘世的束缚。

【English Translation】

Only when thoroughly recognizing the character of one's own nature can one say that one has understood the essence of one's own heart.

Only by thoroughly understanding the common sense of the worldlings can one start discussing the ways to transcend the secular world.

138.　调性谱情　功在其法

138. To adjust your temperament and adapt yourself to the circumstances well depend on the methods to apply.

调性之法，急则佩韦^①，缓则佩弦^②。谱情^③之法，水则从舟，陆则从车。

【中文注释】　①韦：一种柔软的熟皮。
②弦：弓。
③谱情：调谐情绪。此处喻随遇而安或随机应变。

【今文解译】　性子急的佩戴韦，性子慢的佩戴弓，这是调适性情的
方法。
遇到河流就乘船，在陆地上就乘车，这是随遇而安的
做法。

【English Translation】

Wear soft leather if you are an impetuous fellow; wear a bow if you are a slowpoke. — These are the methods to adjust temperament.
Take a boat when on water; take a cart when on land. — These are the ways you accommodate yourself to the circumstances.

139. 好茶涤烦　好酒消忧

139. A good tea can get rid of vexed thoughts while a good wine can dissolve the gloom in the heart.

　　好香用以熏德，好纸用以垂世，好笔用以生花，好墨用以焕彩，好茶用以涤烦，好酒用以消忧。

【今文解译】　好香用来熏染自己的德行，好纸用来承继传世的墨宝，好笔用来书写令人叫绝的文章，好墨用来为烟霞增色加彩，好茶用来涤除心里的烦闷，好酒用来化解胸中的积郁。

【English Translation】

A good burning joss stick is used to nurture the virtue of the burner.

A piece of good paper is used to bear the handwritings worthy of permanent circulation.

A good pen is used to produce elegant writings.

A good ink is used to add luster to drawings.

A good tea is used to get rid of vexed thoughts.

A good wine is used to dissolve the gloom in the heart.

140. 破除烦恼木鱼声　见澈性灵优钵影

140. To get rid of worries, go and listen to the sound of wooden clappers; to penetrate the human nature, go and have a look at the green lotus.

破除烦恼，二更山寺木鱼声；见澈性灵①，一点云堂②优钵影③。

【中文注释】　① 见澈性灵：见澈，洞察。性灵，指人的本性、精神、
性情、情感、智慧等，此处指与佛教较为密切的本性和
智慧。
② 云堂：僧堂，亦作"云房"。此处指寺庙里的禅房。
③ 优钵影：也即优钵罗，梵语，意为青莲花。此处指禅房
里的莲花座。

【今文解译】　要想破除心中的烦恼，不妨去听听二更时分山里寺庙的木
鱼声。
要想洞察人的本性和智慧，不妨去看一眼寺庙禅房里的
莲花座。

【English Translation】

To get rid of your worries, you might as well go and listen to the sound of wooden clappers spreading from a Buddhist temple in the mountain at midnight.

To penetrate the depth of human nature and wisdom, you might as well have a look at the green lotus in the Buddhist monks' abode enveloped in the clouds.

141. 太闲生恶业　太清类俗情

141. Too leisurely a life makes one loose in behavior; too self-contained a deed begets poor taste.

人生莫如闲①，太闲反生恶业②；人生莫如清③，太清反类俗情④。

【中文注释】　　①闲: 悠闲; 闲逸。
②恶业: 不好的事; 坏事或不体面的事。
③清: 清高。
④俗情: 俗套; 落入俗套。

【今文解译】　　人生最享受的莫过于闲逸, 可太过闲逸也会生出不体面的事来。
人生最有品的莫过于清高, 可太过清高反而有点像庸人的俗趣。

【English Translation】

Leisureliness is the top acme of a happy life, but being too leisurely would make one loose in behavior.
Nobility and chastity are most needed in moral cultivation, but if overdone they will be of poor taste.

142. 灵丹一粒　点化俗情

142. A pure and clear mind helps to get rid of vulgarity.

胸中有灵丹一粒，方能点化俗情、摆脱世故。

【今文解译】　自己心里明净了，才能点化世俗的趣味、摆脱世故的缠扰。

【English Translation】

Only by having a pure and clear mind can one release oneself from vulgarities and shake off the fetters of social conventions.

143. 妖冶成泉下骷髅　功名是梦中蝴蝶

143. Beauty can never last and merits are illusive.

　　无端妖冶，终成泉下骷髅；有分功名，自是梦中蝴蝶。

【今文解译】　　美女再怎么妖艳迷人，最终都会变成黄泉下的白骨。
　　　　　　　　功名再怎么应当应分，也只是像梦中蝴蝶那样虚幻。

【English Translation】

A woman, however seductive, will finally become a withered skeleton under the Yellow Springs*.
Merits, no matter how deserved they are, will finally be as illusory as a butterfly in the dream.

【English Annotation】

* The Yellow Springs: Referring to the world of the dead, simply as hell or netherworld.

144. 独坐禅房　意揖达摩

144. Sit alone in the Buddhist abode to gaze at *The Budhidharma Facing to the Wall Painting*.

　　独坐禅房①，潇然无事，烹茶一壶，烧香一炷，凝望达摩面壁图②。垂帘少顷，不觉心静神清，气柔息定，蒙蒙然如混沌境界③，意者揖达摩与之乘槎而见麻姑④也。

【中文注释】　① 禅房：僧徒居住的房屋，泛指佛教寺院。

②《达摩面壁图》：亦称《达摩面壁图轴》，由明代画僧宋旭创作。此图纸本设色，纵 121.3 厘米、横 32.2 厘米，所绘达摩形象古朴而虔诚，四周是野草蓬茸的岩洞，达摩身着红衣，端坐于蒲团之上，正在修行。画心题"问法金銮不顺情，折盖潜向少林行。若无断臂来承受，辜负如来十万程"。署款"庚子新春写于云间超果精舍"。押"宋旭之印""石门山人"二印。

③ 混沌境界：传说中宇宙形成以前模糊一团的景象。

④ 麻姑：又称寿仙娘娘，汉族民间信仰的女神，属于道教人物。

【今文解译】　一人独坐在禅房里，静来无事时，就煮上一壶茶，点起一炷香，凝视《达摩面壁图》。然后闭目，片刻即会觉得心绪平静，神志清爽，气息柔顺，朦朦胧胧仿佛进入了一个混沌的世界，见了达摩就向他作揖叩拜，并与其一起乘坐木筏前去谒见麻姑。

【English Translation】

When not occupied, one may sit alone in the Buddhist abode to brew a pot of tea, light up a burning toss stick, and gaze at *The Budhidharma Facing to the Wall Painting**. Only a little while after closing the eyes, one will become pure and clear of the mind, and soft and calm of the breath, and feeling as if roaming in a free and natural realm, paying respects to Budhidharma and sailing together with him in the same raft to call on Magu*.

【 English Annotation 】

* *The Budhidharma Facing to the Wall Painting*: Budhidharma is an Indian monk who introduced Chan Sect to China towards the end of the Song Dynasty (420-479) of the Southern Dynasties (420-589). The painting was painted by Song Xu (1525-1606?), a famous Buddhist painter of the Ming Dynasty.
* Magu: A female mythical figure in ancient Chinese literature, venerated as a protector of elderly women.

145. 以正敛放　以趣通板

145. Restrain yourself with uprightness and release yourself with interest.

才人之行多放，当以正敛之；正人之行多板，当以趣通之。

【今文解译】　　才华横溢的人，其行为大多桀骜不驯，当用刚直加以约束。

刚正不阿的人，其行为大多古板执拗，当用趣味使之融通。

【English Translation】

A talented guy mostly acts in an unrestrained way; so, one who wants to restrain him should do so with uprightness.

An upright person mostly acts in a restrained way; so, one who wants to make him unrestrained should do so with fun.

146. 疑善信恶　满腔杀机

146. Suspect when aware of philanthropic act and believe when told of wrongdoings, — these are the signs of a dark psychology.

闻人善，则疑之；闻人恶，则信之。此满腔杀机也。

【今文解译】　听说有人做好事却持怀疑态度，听说有人做坏事却深信无疑。这种心理实在是太阴暗了。

【English Translation】

There are persons who become skeptical when aware of another's philanthropic act, and persons who take it as truth when told of someone else's wrongdoings. What a dark psychology!

147. 能脱俗便是奇　不合污便是清

147. Rising above vulgarity is out of the ordinary; never associating with evil elements is unsullied.

能脱俗便是奇，不合污便是清。处巧若拙，处明若晦，处动若静。

【今文解译】　　能超凡脱俗就是不同凡响。
不同流合污就是清纯高雅。
与能人相处要表现得笨拙些。
大庭广众面前切忌显山露水。
环境动荡时一定要保持冷静。

【English Translation】

One who can ever rise above vulgarities is out of the ordinary.
One who never associates himself with the vicious is unsullied.
Pose as dull as you can when among the talented.
Obscure yourself as much as you can when in the place of light.
Not act blindly or recklessly when faced with turbulence.

148. 君子尽心利济　即此便是立命

148. A gentleman establishes his worth and estate by helping others wholeheartedly.

　　士君子①尽心利济，使海内少他不得，则天亦自然少他不得，即此便是立命。

【中文注释】　① 士君子：士君子的含义在古代可有三种解释：一是指上层统治人物，如周制中的卿、大夫或士；二是指有学问且品德高尚的人或学者；三是泛指读书人。

【今文解译】　有品德的君子尽其所能地帮助别人，使世界少不了他，上天也少不了他。——能达到这个境界，人生的意义和价值也就尽显其中了。

【English Translation】

The accomplished gentleman helps others wholeheartedly, and therefore becomes the one the world needs and the heaven needs as well. This is how a gentleman establishes his worth and his estate.

149. 读史耐讹字　闲居耐俗汉

149. To read historical books one has to endure the misspelling words; to live a leisurely life one has to endure the mean fellows.

　　读史要耐讹字，正如登山耐仄路、踏雪耐危桥、闲居耐俗汉、看花耐恶酒，此方得力。

【今文解译】　读史要受得了错别字，正如登山要受得了羊肠小道、踏雪要受得了高耸的桥梁、居家要受得了凡夫俗子、赏花要受得了劣酒，这样才能从中获益。

【English Translation】

To read historical books one has to endure the misspelling words. Equally, to climb a mountain one has to endure the narrow path; to tread the snows one has to endure the towering bridges; to live a leisurely life one has to endure the mean fellows; to appreciate flowers one has to endure the inferior alcohol. Only by doing in this way can one benefit from the reading.

150. 声色娱情　何若净几明窗

150. Seeking pleasures in sensual entertainment is not as good as living a clean, tidy life in peace and ease.

声色娱情，何若净几明窗①，一生息顷。利荣驰念，何若名山胜景，一登临时。

【中文注释】　　① 净几明窗：喻指清净整洁的生活。

【今文解译】　　声色犬马所带来的愉悦，怎比得上几净窗明的生活、一辈子平平安安。
为荣华富贵而绞尽脑汁，怎比得上游历名山胜景、登高望远一览无余。

【English Translation】

Seeking pleasures in sensual entertainment is not as good as living a clean, tidy life in peace and ease.
Racking one's brains to seek glory and wealth is not as good as climbing the beautiful mountains for sightseeing.

151. 心上无事好快活　何必情欲乃为乐

151. Enjoy yourself while you may, and you will be happy right off. Why take love affairs as the sole happiness!

　　若能行乐，即今便好快活。身上无病，心上无事，春鸟是笙歌，春花是粉黛。闲得一刻，即为一刻之乐，何必情欲乃为乐耶？！

【今文解译】　　能行乐的时候就行乐，快活即可获得。对身无残疾、心无烦忧的人来说，春天的鸟鸣就是动听的音乐，春天的花朵就是美丽的女人。有一刻闲暇的时间就享受一刻的快乐，何必只认定男欢女爱才是唯一的快乐？！

【English Translation】

Enjoy yourself while you may, and you will be happy right off. To a healthy body and a carefree heart, the twitters of birds in spring are the same as music and songs, and the brilliance of flowers in spring the same as beautiful women. A moment free from work is the moment worthy of amusement. Why take love affairs as the sole happiness!

152. 兴来醉倒 机息忘怀

152. Drink till drunk when your spirits run high; forget the plots and schemes to keep your heart at ease.

兴来醉倒落花前，天地即为衾枕；机息忘怀磐石上，古今尽属蜉蝣①。

【中文注释】　　① 蜉蝣：一种短命的昆虫。

【今文解译】　　兴致高的时候喝酒，醉了就躺在落花前，把天当作被，把地当作枕。
登临磐石之上，心中的算计尽皆忘却，顿悟古今万物只是蜉蝣而已。

【English Translation】

Drink till drunk when your spirits run high and fall to the ground paved with fallen flowers, just taking the sky as a quilt and the land a pillow.

Banish the plots and schemes from the heart by standing on a big rock, and you will come to realize that all the living creatures are but planktons.

153. 烦恼之场　何种不有

153. In the fair of vexations, there are various vexations.

　　烦恼之场，何种不有，以法眼①照之，奚啻②蝎蹈空花。

【中文注释】　　① 法眼：佛家所认为的五眼之一，指能认识到事物真相的眼力，泛指敏锐深邃的洞察力。
② 奚啻：何止；何不；尽似；尽是。

【今文解译】　　世上什么样的烦恼都有。用佛家的法眼来审视，它们都只不过是趴在"虚幻"这朵花上的蝎子。

【English Translation】

In the fair of vexations, there are various vexations. If observed with an eye of wisdom, they all look like a scorpion sprawling over a visionary flower.

154. 休便休去　了时无了

154. Rest while you may, or you will have no time to do so even if you want to.

如今休去便休去，若觅了时了无时。

【今文解译】　能休息的时候就马上休息，要想等到手头的事都了结了再休息，恐怕是没有尽头的。

【English Translation】

Take a rest when time is available. If you wish to have a rest when all the works in hand are finished, you will never gain your end.

155. 意亦甚适　梦亦同趣

155. Even in their dreams the good companions are also temperamentally compatible.

上高山，入深林，穷回溪幽泉怪石，无远不到。到则拂草而坐，倾壶而醉；醉则更相枕藉以卧。意亦甚适，梦亦同趣。

【今文解译】　登上高山，进入密林，一路阅尽山林里的涧溪、幽泉和怪石，无远不到。停下了大家就席地而坐，以草为垫，倾壶而饮，至醉方休；喝醉了就交替枕着同伴的身体呼呼大睡。心情是何等畅快，即使是在梦里，我们也都意趣相投。

【English Translation】

Ascending the high mountains, going deep into the woods, wandering as far as we can through the winding streams, hidden fountains and strange rocks; when to a stop, sitting straightway on the inclined grasses, drinking with bottoms up till drunk, and then sleeping with our heads pillowed on each other's body in turn; — how merry our hearts, and even in dreams we are also temperamentally compatible!

156. 业净成慧眼　无物到茅庵

156. Remove the sinful intents, and you will gain insight; banish the material desires, and you will refine yourself even in a thatched hut.

业净六根①成慧眼②，身无一物③到茅庵④。

【中文注释】　① 业净六根：六根，通指眼、耳、鼻、舌、身、意，佛家认为这六者是罪孽的根源。业净六根，意即消除这六个罪孽的根源。
② 慧眼：智慧之眼。泛指敏锐的眼力和洞察力。
③ 身无一物：意为毫无牵挂。喻指摒弃一切物欲。
④ 茅庵：草舍，茅庐。

【今文解译】　一旦六根清净，便有了观照世间万物的慧眼。
一旦物欲皆抛，即使置身茅庐也能修身行道。

【English Translation】

Remove the six root sources of sins* completely, and one will naturally have exceptional insight.
Banish the material desires, and one will know how to refine oneself even in a thatched hut.

【English Annotation】

* The six root sources of sins: A Buddhist term referring to eyes, ears, nose, tongue, body and mind.

157. 犬吠鸡鸣　恍似云中世界

157. By listening to the dogs' barking and cocks' crowing, one will feel as if roaming in a cloudy wonderland.

茅帘①外，忽闻犬吠鸡鸣，恍似云中世界②。竹窗下，惟有蝉吟鹊噪，方知静里乾坤。

【中文注释】　　① 茅帘: 茅草编织成的帘子。
　　　　　　　　② 云中世界: 远离尘嚣的世界, 有 "仙境" 之意。

【今文解译】　　茅帘外, 忽然听闻几声鸡鸣狗叫, 恍如自己就徜徉在虚无缥缈的仙境里。
　　　　　　　　竹窗下, 只听得有蝉吟鸦噪之声传来, 这才知道寂静中有个别样的天地。

【English Translation】

Through the thatched curtain, I suddenly hear dogs barking and cocks crowing. All at once I feel as if I am roaming in a cloudy wonderland far away from the human world.

By the bamboo window, only cicadas chanting and magpies crying waft into my ears. Just then I realize that in silence there is another heaven and earth so splendid.

158. 异士未必在山泽

158. The eccentric persons may not dwell in the place among the mountains and rivers.

山泽未必有异士^①，异士未必在山泽。

【中文注释】 ① 异士: 泛指有特殊才华或特异功能的人。

【今文解译】 山谷里河道旁未必有奇异之士, 同样, 奇异之士也未必就住在山谷里河道旁。

【English Translation】

The mountains and rivers may not be the place where the eccentric persons dwell in. Equally, the eccentric persons may not dwell in the place among the mountains and rivers.

159. 可爱之人可怜　可恶之人可惜

159. All the darlings are worthy to be cherished; all the hatefuls only deserve to be regretted.

天下可爱的人，都是可怜人；天下可恶的人，都是可惜人。

【今文解译】　天下可爱的人都是值得怜惜的。
天下可恶的人都是令人惋惜的。

【English Translation】

All the darlings under heaven are the ones who are worthy to be cherished.
All the hatefuls under heaven are the ones who only deserve to be regretted.

160. 急之不白　操之不从

160. There are things one cannot make clear in a hurry and persons who cannot follow what is instructed.

事有急之不白者，宽之或自明，毋躁急以速其忿①；人有操之不从者，纵之或自化，毋操切以益其顽②。

【中文注释】　① 忿：不满；怨恨。此处将其理解成"复杂化"则更为贴切。
② 以益其顽：加剧冥顽不化的程度。

【今文解译】　有些事情越是急于想搞清楚就越是搞不清楚，搁置几天或许会变得清楚起来，千万不要因为情绪急躁而使它们变得复杂化。
有些人你越是想点拨他们，他们就越是不开窍，索性，随他们去，他们或许会有所领悟，切不可操之过急而加剧他们的愚顽。

【English Translation】

Sometimes it is difficult to make things clear in a hurry; but if more time is spared they might be clear of themselves. So, we should not be so impetuous as to make them more complicated.

Sometimes it is hard to make people follow what is instructed; but if less binding is laid they might be moved to action in the end. So, we should not be so impatient as to provoke their stubbornness.

161. 比上不足　比下有余

161. Worse off than some, better off than many.

人只把不如我者较量，则自知足。

【今文解译】　与境况不如自己的人比，人自然也就知道满足了。

【English Translation】

Compared with those whose lot is worse than yours, you will naturally be content with what you have.

162. 俭为贤德　贫是美称

162. To be willing to live a frugal life is a good virtue; to be content with poverty is a good fame.

俭为贤德，不可着意求贤；贫是美称，只在难居其美。

【今文解译】　生活俭朴是一种贤德，但刻意追求这样的贤德就不可取了。

安贫乐道是一种美誉，只是能够受得起这个美誉的人不多。

【English Translation】

To be willing to live a frugal life is a good virtue; but virtue of this kind cannot be designed and sought too purposely.

To be content with poverty is what people highly praise; but the problem is that those worthy of such praise are few.

163. 唤醒梦中之梦　窥见身外之身

163. Wake up from a fancy and stay sober, and one will perceive the essence of human nature.

听静夜之钟声，唤醒梦中之梦[①]；观澄潭之月影，窥见身外之身[②]。

【中文注释】　① 梦中之梦: 中国人自古将人生比作梦。在这里, 前一个"梦"指人生, 后一个"梦"指幻觉中的梦, 即梦幻。
② 身外之身: 佛教用语。第二个"身"是指肉身之外的灵魂, 可引申为人性中的真我。

【今文解译】　夜深人静时聆听寺庙的钟声, 可以把我们从梦幻中唤醒。凝望清澈池塘里的月影, 可以使我们洞见人性中的真我。

【English Translation】

Listen to the sound of a temple bell on a still midnight, and so one will wake up from a fancy and stay sober.
Gaze upon the moon reflection on the surface of a limpid pool, and so one will perceive the essence of human nature.

164. 打透生死关　参破名利场

164. See through the causes of life and death and penetrate the vanity of fame and wealth.

打透生死关，生来也罢，死来也罢。参破名利场，得了也好，失了也好。

【今文解译】　看透了生与死的因果关系，人就会对生死一视同仁。
　　　　　　　参破了名利场的你争我夺，人就会把得失看得很淡。

【 English Translation 】

One will take an equal attitude to the issue of life and death when one perceives the consequences thereof.

One will not be too concerned for personal gains and losses when one penetrates the vanity of fame and wealth.

165. 一笔写出　便是作手

165. A good poet can finish in one breath a poem depicting the landscape before the eye and the appeal in the heart.

作诗能把眼前光景，胸中情趣，一笔写出，便是作手，不必说唐道宋。

【今文解译】　写诗时如能将眼睛所见的景致和心里感受到的情致一气呵成地写出来，便算得上是个有才气的诗人了，不必苛求是否有唐诗宋词的风范。

【English Translation】

A good poet is one who can finish in one breath a poem depicting the landscape before the eye and the emotional appeal in the heart. There is no need to demand if the poem corresponds with the styles of Tang and Song* or not.

【English Annotation】

* Tang and Song: Referring to the dynasties of Tang (618-907) and Song (960-1279), which are known as the best time for poems in the Chinese history.

166. 隐逸林中无荣辱

166. A man who lives as a hermit gives no thought to the personal honor and disgrace.

隐逸林中无荣辱，道义路上无炎凉。

【今文解译】 对于隐逸山林的居士来说，个人的荣耀与耻辱已无须计较。
对于崇尚道义的仁人志士，世态的炎凉无常已不值得关注。

【English Translation】

To live as a hermit in forest, give no thought to personal honor and disgrace.
To seek morality and justice, pay no heed to the fickleness of human affairs.

167. 皮囊速坏　神识常存

167. Human bodies are easy to decay while the power of human intelligence will ever exist.

　　皮囊^①速坏，神识^②常存，杀万命以养皮囊，罪卒归于神识。佛性^③无边，经书有限，穷万卷以求佛性，得不属于经书。

【中文注释】　　① 皮囊：人的肌肤、身体。
　　　　　　　　② 神识：佛家所说的众生的心和识，普遍认为指八识，即：眼、耳、鼻、舌、身、意、末那（梵语 manas 之音译，意识、思量之义）、阿赖耶（梵语 ālaya 之音译，大乘佛教术语，意译为"藏识"，为瑜伽行唯识学派的理论基础之一）等识，可以简单理解为精神力。
　　　　　　　　③ 佛性：佛，指觉悟；性，意为不变。大乘佛教的一些经典认为一切众生皆有佛性，即众生都有觉悟成佛的可能性。佛性一词在不同的情况下有不同的内涵。

【今文解译】　　人的皮囊会很快腐朽，但人的神识却永世长存；杀戮各种动物的生命以滋养人的皮囊，终将归罪于人的神识。人的佛性没有边际，而经书所阐述的佛理却十分有限；通过穷尽万卷经书以求佛性，即使因此而得到了佛性，也跟经书没什么关系。

【English Translation】

Human bodies are easy to decay while the power of human intelligence will ever exist. To slaughter animals to satisfy the need of the human bodies is sinful and will be eventually ascribed to the power of human intelligence.
Man's Buddha-nature is boundless while the Buddhist scriptures are limited in number. To achieve the comprehension of the Buddha-nature by reading through all the scriptures is not the contribution of the scriptures.

168. 闻谤勿怒　见誉勿喜

168. Don't be angry when slandered, nor be complacent when adulated.

闻谤而怒者，谗之隙；见誉而喜者，佞之媒。

【今文解译】　听闻有人诽谤自己就怒不可遏,谗佞的人就会伺机离间。
见到有人恭维自己就喜不自胜,谄媚的人就会乘虚而入。

【English Translation】

If you get angry when slandered, the slanderer will have a loophole to exploit. If you are complacent when adulated, the adulator will break through at a weak point.

169.　人胜我无害　我胜人非福

169. To me, it's neither a hurt if somebody else is one-up on me, nor a blessing if I one-upman somebody else.

人胜我无害，彼无蓄怨之心；我胜人非福，恐有不测之祸。

【今文解译】　别人胜我一筹，并不对我构成什么伤害，因为别人没有理由嫉恨我。

我胜别人一筹，不见得是我的福分，因为这有可能给自己带来麻烦。

【English Translation】

It's not a hurt to me if somebody else is one-up on me, for his one-upmanship won't make him bear a grudge against me.

It's not a blessing to me if I one-upman somebody else, for my one-upmanship might be the cause of trouble in the future.

170. 闭门是深山　读书有净土

170. To take a self-reflection, there is no need to go into the mountains; to read books, no need to find a quiet place.

闭门即是深山，读书随处净土。

【今文解译】　自我反省不必非去深山，关起门来在家里也一样可以做。
读书不必非要找个安静的地方，能读书的地方就是净土。

【English Translation】

To take a self-reflection, one does not have to go and dwell in the depth of mountains, but can do it just indoors.

To read books, one does not have to find somewhere quiet; anywhere fit for reading is the right place.

171. 欲见圣人气象　必须胸中洁净

171. To see the dignified bearing of a sage, one should first make his own heart pure and clear.

欲见圣人气象，须于自己胸中洁净时观之。

【今文解译】　谁要想目睹圣人的仪表风采，首先自己得内心纯净，一无杂念。

【English Translation】

One who intends to see the dignified bearing of a sage can do so only when one has made one's own heart pure and clear.

172. 成名每在穷苦日

172. It often follows that one makes a name for himself when caught in dire straits.

成名每在穷苦日，败事多因得志时。

【今文解译】 　 一个人往往是在身陷困境时成名的，也多在志得意满时衰败的。

【English Translation】

It often follows that one makes a name for himself when caught in dire straits, and declines when all his ambitions are fulfilled.

173. 让利精于取利

173. Surrendering some profits deserved is cleverer than keeping them.

让利精于取利，逃名巧于邀名。

【今文解译】　让利于人要比与人争利更精明。

逃避名声要比争夺名声更聪明。

【English Translation】

Surrendering some profits deserved is cleverer than striving for them.
Evading fame and name is wiser than fighting for them.

174. 求福速祸　泰然得福

174. Calm manner in crisis turns bad fortune into good.

过分求福，适以速祸；安分速祸，将自得福。

【今文解译】　过分地为自己祈求福祉，反而容易招来祸害。
泰然面对突如其来的灾祸，往往能转祸为福。

【English Translation】

Excessive seeking of good fortune accelerates the coming of bad.
Calm manner at a sudden crisis turns bad fortune into good.

175. 看书不可拘泥旧说

175. In reading a book, one should not confine himself to the existing theories.

看书只要理路通透，不可拘泥旧说，更不可附会新说。

【今文解译】　看书贵在将书中的道理融会贯通，不可囿于旧有学说的条条框框，更不可轻易地对新说附会盲信。

【English Translation】

In reading a book, what matters is to get a clear understanding of the substances between the lines. Confining oneself to the existing theories is inadvisable, and more so if lightly chiming in with the new ones.

176. 但识琴中趣　何劳弦上音

176. If you can tell the entertainment in the lute, is there a need to labor your fingers over the strings?

　　对棋不若观棋，观棋不若弹琴，弹琴不若听琴。古云：“但识琴中趣，何劳弦上音？”斯言信然。

【今文解译】　　与人对弈不如观人下棋，观人下棋不如自己弹琴，自己弹琴不如听人弹琴。古语说：“如果识得听琴的乐趣，又何苦自己要劳烦手指去拨弄琴弦呢？”这话有道理。

【English Translation】

Playing chess is no better than watching chess-game; watching chess-game is no better than playing the lute; playing the lute is no better than listening to the lute. There is an old saying which goes: "If you can tell the entertainment in the lute, is there a need to labor your fingers over the strings?" How true the saying!

177. 出一言解之　是无量功德

177. It's an immeasurable merit to forward a suggestion to see others through their difficulties.

　　士君子贫不能济物①者，遇人痴迷处，出一言提醒之，遇人急难处，出一言解救之，亦是无量功德。

【中文注释】　①济物：为人提供物质上的帮助。

【今文解译】　一个因贫寒而不能提供物质帮助的读书人，若能在别人有错还执迷不悟时上前进言提醒一下，或能在别人有急难而一筹莫展时帮着出出主意使其解脱出来，同样也是功德无量的大善举。

【English Translation】

The man of virtue and learning in low water may not in a position to provide economic assistance for his fellow beings. But, when happening upon a person who is obsessed with wrong ideas, if he could say something to show him the right way to follow, or, when happening upon a person who is in a dire peril, if he could forward a suggestion to see him through his difficulty, his deed is also meritorious.

178. 伶人代古人　似今人为文

178. The actors and actresses play the ancients in the way the modern writers create their writings.

伶人代古人语，代古人笑，代古人愤，今文人为文似之。伶人登台肖古人，下台还伶人，今文人为文又似之。假令古人见今文人，当何如愤，何如笑，何如语？

【今文解译】　演员在舞台上表演，说的是古人那时说的话，笑的是古人那时笑的模样，愤慨的是古人那时愤慨的表情，当代文人就是这样写文章的。演员登台演古人，下台后就又做回了自己，这好像也是当代文人作文的套路。若使古人见到当代文人都是这样写东西的，他们又该当如何愤慨，如何笑，如何说话呢？

【English Translation】

The actors and actresses speak, laugh, and express detestation in the way the ancients did; this is the way in which the modern writers write their works. The actors and actresses come on stage to play the ancients and become themselves again after stepping down; this is also the way in which the modern writers do about their writings. If the ancients were made to see how the modern literary men create, what should they do to express detestation, laugh and speak?

179. 闲有余日　正可学问

179. Unoccupied times are the right opportunity for learning and consultation.

夜者日之余，雨者月之余，冬者岁之余。当此三余，人事稍疏，正可一意学问。

【今文解译】　夜晚是一天所剩余的时间，雨日是一月所剩余的时间，冬季是一年所剩余的时间。这三个时间段里人们都比较闲，正可以用来专心做学问。

【English Translation】

Night is the spare time of a day; rainy days, the spare time of a month; winter, the spare time of a year. The three spare times, during which people are usually less occupied, can right be used for learning and consultation.

180. 简傲不可谓高　阿谀不可谓谦

180. Acting with arrogance cannot be regarded as dignity; licking others' boots cannot be regarded as modesty.

简傲不可谓高，谄谀不可谓谦，刻薄不可谓严明，阘茸①不可谓宽大。

【中文注释】　　① 阘茸：阘，庸碌；低劣；茸，鹿茸；细毛。阘茸，泛指人品卑劣或庸碌无能。

【今文解译】　　傲慢无礼并不是尊贵，谄媚奉承并不是谦卑，为人刻薄并不是严明，碌碌无为并不是宽大。

【English Translation】

Acting with arrogance cannot be regarded as dignity.
Licking others' boots cannot be regarded as modesty.
Treating others caustically cannot be regarded as strictness.
Doing nothing cannot be regarded as broad-mindedness.

181. 丹青乃无言之诗　诗句乃有言之画

181. Painting is speechless poetry, poetry is a talking painting.

　　画家之妙，皆在运笔之先，运思之际，一经点染，便减神机。长于笔者，文章即如言语；长于舌者，言语即成文章。昔人谓丹青乃无言之诗，诗句乃有言之画；余则欲丹青似诗，诗句无言，方许各臻妙境。

【今文解译】　画家的灵感都成于挥毫之前，构思的时候稍有分心，他的灵感就会受到影响。长于写作的人，落笔就像说话一样；口齿伶俐的人，说出的话即成文章。古人说，画是无言的诗，诗是会说话的画。而我则希望，画应该有诗的韵味，诗应该超越文字本身。这样，画和诗兴许各自都能达到妙不可言的境界。

【English Translation】

The inspiration of a painter goes before he wields his brush. When working on what and how to present the mood of a painting the painter is not allowed to be distracted, otherwise a minor distraction might result in the loss of the resourcefulness.

He who is well versed in writing can graphically portray what he speaks with succinct words; while he who is well versed in speaking can have chapter at his tongue's tip.

Down the ages paintings have been known as speechless poetry and poetry as paintings able to talk. But I'd rather wish that paintings have the charm of poetry and poetry is beyond language description, thinking that if as wished maybe either of them will reach its own excellent extent.

182. 云霞为侣伴　青松为心知

182. The floating clouds are my companion and the green pines my confidant.

累月独处，一室萧条，取云霞为侣伴，引青松为心知；或稚子老翁，闲中来过，浊酒一壶，蹲鸱①一盂，相共开笑口，所谈浮生闲话，绝不及市朝。客去关门，了无报谢。如是毕余生足矣。

【中文注释】　① 蹲鸱：大芋。因其状如蹲伏的鸱，故称。

【今文解译】　一连数月独居，虽满屋萧条气氛，但仍将云彩视作伴侣，青松视作知己。间或有村里老翁闲中携童前来串门，我便以浊酒、芋头招待之，彼此有说有笑，所谈无非家常，话题绝不涉及市集朝廷。客人走了我便关上门，全然没有"感谢"这样的客套话。能这样度过自己的余生我知足了。

【English Translation】

After several months of staying alone, a roomful of solitude has made the floating clouds as my companion and the green pines as my bosom friend. During the months, the old man of the neighborhood would call on me together with his grandson when at leisure. As the host, I entertained them with a pot of muddling wine and a plate of taro. Together, we chatted and laughed on the subjects merely related to day-to-day life, totally disregarding the affairs of court or those of market. The door would be closed behind the guests as soon as they were sent off, even with no formalities observed between us. I will have nothing to complain if my remaining years could be spent like this.

183. 耳目宽则天地窄

183. Too many desires of the ears and eyes make the heaven and earth narrow.

耳目宽则天地窄，争务短则日月长。

【今文解译】　耳目之欲太多，天地的空间就会变得狭窄。

少一点名利心，日子就会过得清闲而悠长。

【English Translation】

Too many desires of the ears and eyes make the space between heaven and earth narrow.

Less ambition to seek fame and gain enables one to live a long life in a leisurely way.

184. 江水汨汨　疑有湘灵

184. The murmuring stream raises one up to believe that there are goddesses in the water picking the strings.

从江干溪畔，箕踞石上，听水声浩浩潺潺，㶁㶁冷冷，恰似一部天然之乐韵，疑有湘灵①在水中鼓瑟也。

【中文注释】　① 湘灵：传说的湘水之神，即舜帝的妃子娥皇和女英姐妹俩。娥皇、女英是上古时期汉族神话传说中的人物，尧帝的两个女儿，也称"皇英"。长曰娥皇，次曰女英，姐妹同嫁舜帝为妻。有一次舜帝巡视南方，娥皇、女英追踪至洞庭湖，闻舜帝死于苍梧之野，二妃往寻，泪染青竹，竹上生斑，因称"潇湘竹"或"湘妃竹"。二妃也死于江湘之间。自秦汉时起，湘江之神湘君与湘夫人的爱情神话被演变成舜与娥皇、女英的传说。

【今文解译】　大河的支流岸边，我盘腿坐在石头上，聆听流水的声音，时而浩浩，时而潺潺，时而㶁㶁，时而冷冷，宛若一部浑然天成的音乐剧，隐隐之中觉得娥皇、女英两位妃子就在水中拨弦弹琴。

【English Translation】

Beside the brook of a big river I sit cross-legged on a rock to listen to the sound of the limpid water now roaring now murmuring, just like a melody performed by Nature, which succeeds in raising me up to believe that there are goddesses in the water picking the strings.

185. 有书癖而无剪裁　徒号书橱

185. One who has a hobby to collect books but does not know how to make a professional selection is only a bookcase.

有书癖①而无剪裁②，徒号书橱③；惟名饮④而少蕴藉⑤，终非名饮。

【中文注释】　① 书癖：对书籍的特别爱好。此处指有收集书籍嗜好的人。

② 剪裁：此处喻挑选或筛选。

③ 徒号书橱：徒有其名的书橱。此处可解读为"只是个放书的书橱"。

④ 名饮：本文后半部分出现两个名饮，前一个名饮意为"惟名酒是饮"，后一个意为"懂酒的饮者"。

⑤ 蕴藉：可理解为（酒里）所蕴含的文化。

【今文解译】　有书癖但对收集什么样的书却不做任何甄选，这样的人纯粹就是个书橱。

只喜欢喝名酒但不知道名酒的文化底蕴，这样的人终究不是懂酒的饮者。

【English Translation】

One who has a hobby to collect books but does not know how to make a professional selection is only a bookcase.

One who is keen on drinking branded liquid but knows nothing about the culture in it can never be a good drinker.

186. 鸟啼花落　有会于心

186. The crying of birds and the falling of flowers are pleasant to a knowing heart.

鸟啼花落，欣然有会于心，遣小奴，挈瘿樽①，酤白酒，饮一梨花瓷盏，急取诗卷，快读一过以咽之，萧然不知其②在尘埃间也。

【中文注释】　① 瘿樽：瘿，长在楠树上的树瘤，质地坚硬。瘿樽，用楠木瘤做成的盛酒器具。
② 其：此处指所读的诗或诗所描写的意境。

【今文解译】　听到鸟的啼鸣，看到花的飘落，心里因有所呼应而欣喜不已，忙不迭差侍童带着酒瓮买酒去，一口饮尽斟在梨花瓷酒盏里的酒，急切地取来诗卷打开，飞快地将它读完，没曾想滚滚红尘竟还有这等诗境。

【English Translation】

When gladly arriving at a fresh understanding of the crying of birds and the falling of flowers, I sent my boy to fetch me strong liquid with a wooden flagon. After a cup of wine, a porcelain cup painted with pear-flowers, I unfolded the poetry scroll in a hurry and read it through speedily in one breath, and couldn't help admiring that this dusty world would have such a poetic presentation.

187. 山峦之胜　妙于天成

187. The attraction of a mountain is mostly brought forth by Nature.

自古及今山之胜，多妙于天成，每坏于人造。

【今文解译】　自古及今，凡名山胜景的绝妙之处大多成于天然，但却每每毁于人工修建带来的破坏。

【English Translation】

From ancient times till now, the attraction of a mountain has been mostly brought forth by Nature, while the ruin of it by manual constructions in many cases.

188. 清闲无事　坐卧随心

188. Those unoccupied and having nothing to do are enabled to sit or sleep at will.

清闲无事，坐卧随心，虽粗衣淡饭，但觉一尘不染。忧患缠身，繁扰奔忙，虽锦衣厚味，只觉万状苦愁。

【今文解译】　　闲来无事时，要坐要躺全由自己高兴，虽然只是粗衣淡饭，但还是觉得这样才无忧无虑。

忧患缠身的人为逐利而四处奔波，尽管是锦衣玉食，但还是觉得这样活在世上实在太累。

【English Translation】

Those unoccupied and free to sit or sleep at will, though clad in coarse clothes and fed with scanty meals, are enabled to enjoy the carefree hours.

Those entangled in troubles and busy making money, though supplied with beautiful dresses and fine food, are undergoing sufferings in every way.

189. 舞蝶游蜂　落花飞絮

189. Full of imagination are the dancing butterflies and roaming bees as well as the fallen petals and flying catkins.

舞蝶游蜂，忙中之闲，闲中之忙；落花飞絮，景中之情，情中之景。

【今文解译】　飞舞的蝴蝶和漫游的蜜蜂，它们忙碌的时候像是闲着，闲着的时候像在忙碌。

随风飘落的花瓣和飞扬的柳絮，它们既是景色中的情致，又是情致中的景色。

【English Translation】

The dancing butterflies and roaming bees seem to be at leisure while working hard, and hard-working while at leisure.

The fallen petals and flying catkins are the reflection of the mood amid the scene, and the scene amid the mood as well.

190. 鸟栖高枝　士隐岩穴

190. Birds like to perch on high branches while hermits prefer to dwell in the cave.

鸟栖高枝，弹射难加；鱼潜深渊，网钓不及；士隐岩穴，祸患焉至？！

【今文解译】　　鸟栖息在高高的枝头，弹弓射不到它们。
鱼潜游在深深的水底，网钩够不着它们。
修士隐居岩穴，祸患又怎能伤害到他们？！

【English Translation】

Birds perch on high branches, so no one can shoot them.
Fish dive deep in the water, so no one can net or hook them.
Hermits dwell in the cave, so how can mishap harm them?

191. 混迹尘中　高视物外

191. See beyond the material world while going through its hubbub.

混迹尘中，高视物外；陶情杯酒，寄兴篇咏；藏名一时，尚友千古。

【今文解译】　人虽在滚滚红尘之中，但眼光要超然物外。
在酒杯中陶冶情操，于吟咏中寄托意趣。
暂且隐姓埋名，以求先在精神上与古人契合。

【English Translation】

See beyond the material world while going through its hubbub.
Foster your temperament in wine and confine your interest in poetry.
Hide your identity for a time so as to correspond to the mood of the ancients.

192. 五夜鸡鸣　一觉睡醒

192. The crows of a cock early in the morning wake me up from a deep sleep.

五夜鸡鸣，唤起窗前明月；一觉睡醒，看破梦里当年。

【今文解译】　五更时分，雄鸡报晓，只见一轮明月高挂在窗外的天际。刚被唤醒的我，已然看破当年那些梦幻般的往事。

【 English Translation 】

The crows of a cock early in the morning, the moment the bright moon is still illuminating on the windows, wake me up from a deep sleep and enable me to reflect and penetrate the dream-like past.

193. 取凉于扇　汲水于井

193. A fan fetches cool; well water quenches thirst.

取凉于扇，不若清风之徐来；汲水于井，不若甘雨之时降。

【今文解译】　用扇子扇出来的风不如徐徐吹来的清风那么凉爽。
从井里打上来的水不如时时降临的雨水那么甘甜。

【English Translation】

The wind brought about by a fan is not as cool as that slowly produced by fresh air.

The water drawn from a well is not as sweet as that delivered by a shower now and then.

194. 飞凌缥缈　坐看氤氲

194. Set your mind in the world of illusions by sitting yourself to watch the mists, gathering and dispersing.

月榭^①凭栏，飞凌缥缈^②；云房^③启户，坐看氤氲^④。

【中文注释】　① 月榭：月光映照下的台榭。
　　　　　　② 飞凌缥缈：飞扬飘忽之意。
　　　　　　③ 云房：佛殿，佛堂。亦称"云堂"。
　　　　　　④ 氤氲：迷漫而飘荡的云烟雾气。

【今文解译】　融融的月光下，身体倚着台榭的栏杆，心神已然飘向了虚无。
　　　　　　推开佛殿大门，坐看满山的云烟雾气依依袅袅、奔腾翻卷。

【English Translation】

Leaning on the rails of a moon-lit terrace, I feel as if my thoughts were wafting to the world of illusions.
Opening the gate of a temple atop the cloudy mountain, I sit myself to watch the mists, gathering and dispersing.